Endorsements

Will's book is a special testimony that is raw, authentic, and heartwarming which is very hard to find in literature these days. He captured the essence of what it is to grow up in a challenging and dysfunctional environment and then find spiritual guidance by falling in love with his soul mate Amy. Will's walk with the Lord is one few men can claim, but many strive to obtain. I am one of those. Will's book spoke to my heart as we both have had similar life stories with our youth and then our chosen military profession. Combat and doing dangerous missions and the adrenaline that comes with it is like a drug that provides you with a "high" you crave and need to keep getting. More often than not, our families suffer through our "deployment highs" and we don't understand the pain we are causing them as we do our missions for God and country. Will does an outstanding job explaining this process and all the physical and emotional highs, lows, drama, and trauma that go with. The one constant in all of this that Will falls back on was our faith in God and the Lord Jesus Christ. Will's book provides real life experiences of how to do things right as well as how things should not be done. He shows us how important it is to believe in Jesus and stay in faith, even during the darkest of times. As I feverishly read Will's book I found myself understanding more about my own life's struggles and how important my renewed walk with Christ is. All of us can learn something from <u>Where I Belong</u> and I found reading it provided healing for my troubled soul. Semper Fi.

~John M. Allison, Sr. (Lt. Col., USMC, Ret.)

I finished the book last night - and I loved it! What a great read - the stories that you told, the message you conveyed, all of it - just great. I had no idea of the back story, had no idea of what it led to, had no idea it was your father and that you were estranged for so long. I'm glad that was in the book. It's strange how people come into your life at certain times. You had a big impact on all of us. When you shared of your experience, I was blown away - and the main message you had after doing all those amazing things was that you were just trying to be "Super William" chasing things that really didn't matter in the long run. I look forward to book #2!

~ Nick B., Asst. Disctrict Attorney, Asheville, NC

Well, it's 1:30AM... I should be asleep, but I'm awake, because I finally got the time and simply HAD to finish your book.
And I have to share (because I'm a little teary eyed - in a good way) and just say what a beautiful life story you have. I'm so thankful you've decided to share your story and God's glory with the world and I'm so thankful to have met you. If I ever wrote a book about my life, you would be a key instrumental person in it!

~ Amanda D., devoted wife, mother & entrepreneur

I was reminded of the song For By Your Grace by Rita Baloche while reading this book. This was a very painful, honest account of your life and the challenges you faced running from your past to find yourself. It is true, you can run from God but you cannot hide! Thank you for your sacrifices and courage while serving in the military and also for your compassion without diminishing your morals and character. I also came to understand more fully the sacrifices of our military families. A parent maintaining the household and raising the children are challenging enough, not to mention the worry of where the loved one will be deployed next, or even when and if they will get to see their loved one again. It really hit home, that not only do we need to lift our service men and women in prayer but also their families. Thank you for sharing a message of hope and redemption and may we never forget...we are all worth it because God chose us!

~ Wanda B., business professional

Where I Belong (A Journey Declassified) is anything but your typical read of a Christian testimony book. Will has masterfully penned a reflection and glimpse into his soul and takes us readers into a journey so raw and transparent that it truly touches the deepest part of our soul that needs encouragement and ferocious freedom by replacing lies with truth, allowing us to better live life at home as well as overseas downrange.

I'm a better person and fellow warrior from knowing Will, Amy, and their family for nearly 25 years. Both our families understand struggle, challenges and injustices that apart from the Power of the Word of God and a loving Heavenly Father, would not be possible to overcome. He redeems our failures as well as others in our life and uses them for great and mighty outcomes — that is the life of Will Cunningham. I encourage you to not only to read this unique outlier warrior's book, but get an extra copy because you will want others to read it as well!

~*Victor Marx, President of All Things Possible Ministries*

When life becomes routine and down right exhausting from chasing things that fade in value, have you asked, "how can we escape this sense of "meaningless" existence and move to a life that has meaning?" Have you ever thought, "If life is "meaningless," then what I do, and the choices I make really don't matter?" Or do they?

Here is a man who overcame hardships of life and learned how to honor God. Somewhere along the way in his middle adult years, he got way off course and wasted years of his life, turning his back on God while chasing the wind. He had the Solomon Syndrome. It was as if he spent those years climbing the wrong mountain trying to find fulfillment and satisfaction, only to get to the place he had hoped to arrive and find his climb was "meaningless". He learned some painful lessons the hard way and ultimately learned that God doesn't waste a life, but devises a means for those that are abandoned to come back to him, where they belong.

If you are middle-aged or older, this book should resonate with you. If you're a young adult, and wonder if you are chasing the "meaningless," this book is worth your read.

If you are younger – please listen, because this story can give you a
good head start and save you from a lot of confusion and heartache.

~ Dr. James Walker, Lead Pastor
Lake Hills Community Church, Candler, NC.

———————

I just finished your book, *Where I Belong*, and it was a huge blessing. You
are a good writer! Thanks for sharing your story so openly and thanks too
for your heart for God and the kingdom.

~ Durwood Snead, Director of Global-X, North Point Church

———————

Just finished your book. Your life experiences, especially in military and
civilian intelligence gathering, gives you a great platform to write from,
and made me want to keep reading. The most important thing, of course
was your recounting of how God has pursued and is pursuing you, and
working through you for His purposes and glory.

~Tom McPeak, Ph.D. Economic Development Consulting, LLC

———————

I didn't want to wait any longer to let you know how much I enjoyed
the book. On a personal level I just thank the Lord for His Grace and what
he has done and is doing in your lives. Wow! The book is a great read.
Felt like I was reading a Tom Clancy novel. I had to keep reminding
myself that it was William who was the person in the story. And I was very
blessed to have even been mentioned in your story. I think your story has
great potential to help communicate that message. God does not give up on
us even when we have given up on ourselves. Amy, God bless you for
never giving up on Will. Super thankful for you guys and pray that God
will continue to bless.

~ Tim Newman, Pastor of Calvary Chapel Winward, Hi

———————

I have known Will and Amy Cunningham for over 20 years. Most of my
contact with them was in the context of our local church, Calvary Chapel

in Honolulu. My simple observation of this couple was that they seemed to me to be quiet, humble, unassuming and hard workers in the church. This remained my viewpoint until I read the manuscript for "Where I Belong".

Will's book told of course from his own perspective chronicles the ups and downs of a guy who, much to my surprise was very much involved in the intelligence community in the military. Then he had his own inherent struggles with faith that was being tested on a regular basis.
Fast forward. Will goes to North Carolina and has become one of the key leaders in his town helping the poor, marginalized and homeless be able to find meaning and purpose in their lives as he helps assist a local rescue mission there in the city of Asheville. He then expands that same heart globally, helping refugees and displaced Syrians living in Lebanon's farmlands with the organization Heart For Lebanon. He continued with successfully opening a private Christian counseling practice where he helps those broken in their spirit.

This book will be a God send for anyone who thinks that God is not the god of a second, and third chance! Will has experienced the love of God as a recipient but also has been a channel for the grace of God to many people to look to him for leadership in his present ministry. I commend this book to you especially if you're struggling with forgiving yourself for past failures or hurts that others have inflicted on you. If you follow Will's example you won't blame others, God or the devil for your issues but you will face your very real issues with the truth of God's Word, by His grace make the necessary changes, as Will did, and you will find victory.

Many have somehow not been able to comprehend that God is truly a "Hound of Heaven" chasing you down simply out of his passionate love for you to bring you in, (or back as the case may be) to his kingdom.
~ *Danny Lehmann, International Dean, University of the Nations,*
Youth With A Mission

Where I Belong

A Journey, Declassified

By

William Cunningham

DEDICATION

My wife Amy, who has shown me more grace that is heaven made and that I ever knew existed. "You get me!"

To my children:

Christian, the silent hero, a soldier & paratrooper, one who has been knocked down in the ring of life yet ignores the critics and keeps standing up fighting.

Elizabeth, the missionary & lover of the poor in spirit, who has shown me humility and confidence and when to use them. Thank you for helping me smile again.

Blake, operator & marine, who has forgiven me more than I thought I deserved and has shown me that success comes from much failure.

Kevin, the confident, the calm, the collected. You forged through the disappointments of life, against all odds proved what it means to press on.

To the many friends who listened, to counseling clients who allowed me to speak into their lives and people I have chatted with along the way.

Where I Belong

ACKNOWLEDGMENTS

First, to my opening editor, LaRue Neilson, who cleaned me up more than I know and provided valuable support along the way. You are a true friend.

Second, to Jane Prevost, LPC, Ed. S, my inside editor, who evaluated the highs and lows of my life and gave valuable feedback. Thank you for inspiring me and believing my story is worth sharing.

Third, to my closing editor and word-smith, Megan Vengala, you have endured my imperfection, my impatience and my impolite nagging. Thank you for your careful re-tooling of my words.

Fourth, to my eldest son, Christian, who encouraged me to be patient and finish well with the final touches of this 5-year project. You are a scholar in your own right. Thanks for taking the time to listen to classical music by the fire and helping me cross the finish line.

Finally, to the voice of reason, my wife, who is the assistant chief editor of my life and the greatest woman I have ever known. You get me!

COVER DESIGN BY ROBIN LUDWIG DESIGN INC.
WWW.GOBOOKCOVERDESIGN.COM

Where I Belong

FOREWORD
(A Note From The Editor)

I want to begin by thanking Will and Amy for the privilege to be a part of their story. I am honored to have been a part of this book in a small way. Will asked me to share with you what I gained as I did the initial edit on this book. As I have reflected on this, I am going to share with you five "challenges" I was given having read this book of their story.

First - just as I suspected and have now confirmed - Will is super lucky because Amy is a **Saint**.

All joking aside, I came away convinced of the value of **Support** – a cheerleader, a person in your court, someone who says, "you can" and means it, who stands beside you when others doubt. For Will, that person is Amy. While Will lived this story, Amy supported him. She persevered through long absences, lots of moves, career changes, single parenting and the many other duties the spouses of those in the military must perform, oftentimes alone. I am sure I speak on behalf of Will when I say thank you Amy (his wife) for showing what it means to unconditionally support someone you love.

Second, as I read this book I realized how important it is to **Share your story**. You see, the Bible tells us God crafted Will's story before time began. Not one event in this book happened by accident. Every encounter in Will's life was designed to bring him to a personal relationship with Christ. As we were discussing some of the edits, Will shared with me how difficult it was for him to share this story. And yet, it is in the telling we meet grace and God reminds us that in sharing we invite others to the foot of the cross.

Third, this book reminded me to be a **Seeker**. Woven throughout the adventures on the high sea, the intel and classified operations, the transitions, the high and low places, Will remained consistent in seeking God's better plan. His story encourages the reader to be wary of the status quo – to be mindful of the admonition throughout God's Word that those who seek the Lord's face will find Him.

Inevitably, if one is a seeker then at some point there must be **Submission**. As Will's story so beautifully portrays, submission is born out of an act of the will and not of the heart. Will teaches that submission is an act of obedience and to walk in obedience to God is to love God.

And finally, one cannot leave Will's story without feeling a call to **Serve**. Service to others is a tangible, feet on the ground expression of love. Running throughout the theme of this book is Will's calling to serve – to serve our country, to serve his family, to serve his church, to serve his friends and comrades, to serve others less fortunate than himself. As a reader, you are invited to serve and experience God's faithfulness.

In 1 Timothy Paul taught the foundational commands to Timothy's call into God's service. He instructed Timothy that in recalling these commands it would serve as a reminder to him and to others that follow to fight the battle well and to hold on to the faith. Will, thank you for sharing your story with us. As you recall God's story for your life, you remind us to fight the battle well and to hold on to the faith because God is always faithful to bring us home where we belong.

~ LaRue Neilson

TABLE OF CONTENTS

	Dedication	Pg 9
	Acknowledgments	Pg 11
	Foreword	Pg 13
1	Logistical Replenishment (Log-Rep)	Pg 17
2	Secret Agent Man	Pg 29
3	Patching The Pain	Pg 39
4	Making Commitments	Pg 49
5	Port Calls	Pg 57
6	Grass Is Not Greener On the Other Side	Pg 65
7	Awarded	Pg 73
8	VWs & Porsches	Pg 79
9	Digging Ditches	Pg 91
10	Back In Intel	Pg 99
11	Heroes	Pg 131
12	Honey-Pot	Pg 153
13	The Darker Side: "You have to come home"	Pg 159
14	F.O.C.	Pg 165
15	The Only Thing You Can Do To Help Yourself Is To Change Your Life	Pg 169
16	A Pivotal Day	Pg 173
17	Just As I Am	Pg 183
18	You Are Addicted To Yourself	Pg 195
19	T.R.U.S.T (Amy's Perspective)	Pg 203
20	Where I Belong - (Do you want to be made well – John 5)	Pg 207
	Bio: William Cunningham	Pg 219

Where I Belong

Chapter 1

LOGISTICAL REPLENISHMENT

(LOG-REP)

The carrier group was cutting through waves in the southern portions of the Sea of Japan, bearing 180 (one eight zero) degrees southbound toward the Philippine Sea. The shipboard personnel were about the plan of the day working in their different departments. As an intelligence specialist, I was caught between thousands of filmed image files taken by the SR-71 Blackbird in a classified storage locker toward the forward bow of the ship. One of many collateral duties, I had to file highly classified images in a sequential order. With our carrier group were several other ships, including one of two battle ships left in the US inventory at the time, the USS Missouri (the Mighty Mo). There was also our flagship, the USS Blue Ridge, where the admiral commanded the task force. Our group was called Group Alpha.

As the summer heat beat down on the ocean and bounced back up on the 40,000+ tons of steel hull of the carrier USS Midway, over the 1MC loud speaker was heard, "Snoopy Team, Snoopy Team to the flight deck. I say again, Snoopy Team, Snoopy Team to the flight deck!" This was my cue. I locked up the file room and ran toward the ops center located in the middle of the ship. I had about 15 minutes to navigate my way through numerous knee knockers (compartmented passageway hatches that were shin length high) to get into the OZ Division (intelligence department), put on my flight suite, grab my 35mm camera, and check in with the intel officer on what the scenario was.

Lt. Commander Johnson, a redheaded, light-complected guy was already standing in front of a center map console. Petty Officer 2nd class St. Jon was briefing the commander on a maritime intel report that had come in and was showing him where we believed a hostile Russian vessel had departed. He outlined its heading along with projected speed to indicate how the vessel had caught up with our battle group. As St. Jon continued, more personnel were gathering around the center map console when finally, the question I wanted answered was asked, "Do we know what type of vessel it is?" Unfortunately, the report did not indicate the type, just that it was a Russian destroyer that had departed from the port of Petropavlovsk at a specific date.

As I was collecting the last bit of information and strapping on my flight gear, I checked my camera settings and heard the rotors of the SH 3 Sea-King helo propel. I looked at the commander and told him, "I got what I needed," and began to make my way to the flight deck. As the commander was following me, he said, "Cunningham, you know the drill." I popped in and said, "Sir, I got it! Shoot 8-point photography and..." He popped back and said, "No, be safe up there." I remarked back to him, "Aye sir."

By this time, we had reached the flight deck which had been heated up by the sun. We felt the wind from the helo blades blowing down on us as well as from the ship pulling in the ongoing wind as it was moving at more than 25 knots through the water. Yellow and green shirts (air wing personnel) were moving about the flight deck in a fluster of busy work. The flight deck was always a dangerous place on the carrier, especially during operations which were ongoing almost 24/7. Just a few nights before, I was awakened at 0345 by Chief Vanknockan, a white-haired, salty sailor. One of the other collateral duties I held was EAM officer. EAM stands for Emergency Action Message which is a drafted report sent to key leadership of major incidents. On that morning, I had to draft an EAM on a downed aircraft. One of our EA-6B Prowler aircraft was conducting low-level flight ops when a wave swelled up and tipped the aircraft causing it to dive deep in the sea. There were four pax (personnel) on board and they were never found. Therefore, the last thing the commander wanted was his EAM officer to go down on a routine maritime surveillance op.

With my camera wrapped around my neck and shoulder, I sat on the side of the helo doorway with my feet hanging and reached for the safety harness to lock myself in. The harness enabled me to have plenty of slack so that I could lean out and take the needed shots of my target. I always gave it plenty of slack as I did not like to be constrained. I put my flight helmet on, turned my head to the left toward the pilot, raised my hand up, and gave him the circle motion indicating, "Let's go!" As the bird lifted I gave my commander a fast salute.

Our target was a combatant ship roughly 3 to 5 miles due northeast of our location. The helo buzzed with numerous electronics. The pilot and navigator were exchanging chatter over the coms, checking and reporting location and flight status. As we began to approach the vessel, I flipped my mic on and requested that the pilot give me a quick fly around so that I could assess how I was going to shoot pictures of the vessel. He piped back and said, "Alright, but just to remind you, we cannot conduct any direct fly-overs!" I commented back, "Romeo-Lima-Charlie." That means, "Read you Loud and Clear." Fly-overs on a maritime vessel were against US rules of engagement (ROE), and if intentional, could ignite a conflict on international waters.

The pilot flew the sea-king around on the first pass as I requested, allowing me to get a good look and set my camera to shoot. I flipped on my mic again and looked at the pilot and gave him my hand motion whirl again and told him, "It's show time! Take it slow!" This time I began to shoot the vessel from the starboard side, then fantail quarter, then fantail, then other fantail quarter, then port side, then port bow quarter then bow, and finally starboard side bow quarter, completing my 8-point shots. Just to be sure that I had enough, I shot a bunch of shots as we were leaving the vicinity. Amid shooting my last shots, the helo took a sharp, unexpected turn, tilting the aircraft 15 or so degrees, thrusting me out the doorway. I held on to the camera in one hand and grabbed hold of the harness, trying to wrap my arm into it, but it was too late. I was already outside the helo doorway dangling just a few feet from the entry. I had no problem climbing back in. As I was pulling myself up on the door landing, I flipped on my mic and yelled out, "What the *#$% was that all about!" The pilot, the navigator, and the crew member were laughing their heads off. The pilot came back and said, "We couldn't help ourselves! You intel boys get too comfortable up here taking your happy snaps!" Cussing under my breath, I just piped back "Romeo-Lima-Charlie, LT. Let's get back to the ship and see what we got!"

Within minutes of flying back to the carrier, the pilot pops back over the mic and tells me that we have another vessel that OZ wants me to check out. It was two miles east and almost a parallel heading from the Russian destroyer that I just finished taking pictures of. I piped back at the pilot and said, "Let's do it, same drill!"

As we made our approach to the vessel, I was unable to make out the ship until I got closer. I was trained to identify merchant ships by their kingposts, masts and bridge placement. However, this particular ship almost seemed to be a floating block of steel from the distance we were flying. When we got closer I could see the draped cargo and began to take my shots, again shooting all 8 points and then finishing off the roll of film as we departed the vicinity.

Once back on the flight deck I excitedly made my way down to the on-board photo lab where I met PH2 Carl Tate. Carl was a photo mate, 2nd class. A real good guy. He loved his job and being down away from everyone else. I handed off my camera and told him, "Whatever you do, don't give this up to anyone. Call me and we will make selections when they are ready." Surveillance photos were like gold in those days. The reason why is that they got us intel guys noticed, especially if we could explain what we shot. That was a key. It gave us a chance to be in front of the Old Man, the captain of the ship.

I made my way back up to OZ Division. A flurry of activity was buzzing around. You could hear flight ops going on with F-18s taking off, tie-down chains being dropped on the steel flight deck to secure helos and sailors in my section running down information. I made my way to several binders where we maintain our Naval Maritime Intelligence Reports.

First, I wanted to look up the last vessel I shot. I remembered it's bridge was more aft, it had a mast kingpost, and it was a cargo carrier. Believe it or not, all that was important. CCAMKKK was the code for the type of cargo ship, which would tell me size, weight displacement, and so on. Next was the flag it flew, which was a Panamanian flag. This was a problem as the majority of foreign ships registered their vessels in Panama, so they could escape large insurance coverages. However, Lords of London, a major insurance provider for vessels, kept very good records of who registered in Panama as well as other places. Luckily, I also had the name of the ship (I took note of it while shooting pictures of the fantail), which helped tremendously. It was named Ohostk. Jotting all this down, I began my intel research going through GENSER intel reports to see if this ship was mentioned anywhere. Sure enough, it was reported leaving a North Korean port just a couple of days before.

Next was the Russian destroyer. While in intel school, we had to memorize most of the Russian armament. We also had to get familiar with what ports had what class of vessels. Petropavlovsk was primarily a sub base with two known classes of destroyers. One was the Udaloy and the other was the Sovremenny. The photos were going to reveal what was on the water behind us. Before heading down to the photo lab I had to map out what I knew about these vessels, where they came from, what their bearings were, and where they were heading. As I drew out on the map bearing and heading lines, I had Petty Officer St. Jon check my numbers. Then I asked him, "What do you think? I am thinking IO." He agreed, the Indian Ocean. I needed to get the photos back and see if my hunch was right.

The photo lab had all the pictures done. As I spread them out on the console and began to study the images from all the different angles that were shot, I could quickly pick up what Russian destroyer it was that we believed was trailing our carrier group, Udaloy class. The Udaloy class had a distinctive signature on the side of the ship that looked like an upside down "U" covering the missile bay area, unlike the Sovremenny, which does not have a covering for the missile bay. The cargo ship peaked my interest, as it caused me to study the goods it covered on the cargo deck. After looking at multiple angles, the cargo began to pop out of a large crate with a gun turret protruding out. Then I noticed a partial fuselage with rotors on the end. This cargo ship was carrying military grade arms, and not just any type of arms, but Russian arms.

Having this arms carrier, a couple of miles off our wake changed the scope of what we were thinking. The Udaloy was not surveilling us as we suspected. It was providing protective escort for the cargo carrier. This was a huge deal as the US had imposed an arms embargo for several countries. The sixty-four-thousand-dollar question was where these vessels were heading.

It was 1987, and the Russian occupation in Afghanistan was seeing it's last days. The Soviets had spent 10 years in that country destroying it in hopes to take it over and spread their communist philosophies. They ended up exiting a year later in 1988 after the US lent support to the Mujahideen. Now mostly Taliban supplied weapons through clandestine channels. During the height of the Soviet's Afghan occupation, the CIA had also determined that it would try to sell military grade arms to Iran to deter or block any furtherance of Soviet influences in the Middle East and other Persian Gulf states. Graham Fuller, a CIA analyst, suggested this to Director William Casey who then took it to Congress. The suggestion did not go over well and was denied. The US and Iran relations were still strained over the assassination of the Shah and the Embassy hostage situation. The problem was, this "No Go" decision opened opportunities for the Soviets. Since we did not move on selling arms to Iran, the Soviets did. Not only did they flood the region with military arms, they signed agreements to train the Iranian secret intelligence agency, SAVAMA. This organization was intended to replace the SAVAK who was the intelligence agency under the Shah of Iran. The purpose was to get rid of the western influenced intelligence agency and slip in the Soviet trained elements.

Through other collection platforms we learned what we needed to know and answered the sixty-four-thousand-dollar question. This arms carrier was making its way to an Iranian port or an allied state to transport the arms to one of their bases. Commander Johnson was prompted to pop into our intel shop for an update. "Commander, this is what we have so far. The Russian combatant is a Udaloy Destroyer which departed in the early a.m. out of Petropavlovsk sub base. Two days before, a Panamanian cargo ship named Ohostk left the North Korean port of Pangyon and was later picked up trailing the cargo ship by the Udaloy. Furthermore, sir, we believe the cargo ship is carrying Russian military grade arms with a destination to Iran."

The commander piped back, "Let me get this straight. You are telling me that a Russian destroyer departed from a Soviet submarine port to pick up a Panamanian registered cargo vessel that departed from a North Korean port two days ago carrying Russian military arms to deliver them to some port in Iran. Is that about the gist of it?" "Yes sir," I replied with a bit of doubt in my voice. He asked what led us to this hypothesis. We then showed him the intelligence pictures and reports. He stood there with his hand rubbing his chin and said, "I get it." With some surprise, I replied to him with a little excitement, "Roger that, sir. Are you ready for us to take this up to the Old Man?" He gave me the green light to move forward and show the pictures to the Captain on the bridge. Once he was okay with the images and gist, I could come back and draft up an intel report that would go out to the following agencies: ONI, CINCPACFLT, DIA and CIA, along with others in our battle group.

I packaged the draft MIR (Maritime Intel Report) along with pictures and made my way up to the bridge to see the skipper. While adjusting my uniform, checking my military bearing and rehearsing in my head what I needed to report to the skipper, I began to think, "What if I am wrong?" This was always an issue. Intelligence work is never an exact science. Never. Our discovery would go through classified channels to all the spook agencies and eventually end up either in a White House Briefing or the Executive Morning Summary to the president. Our piece was small. Our initial draft intelligence report would later be fully evaluated by higher agencies and they, in turn, would initiate their own analyst, foreign assets, and other operatives to collect any other needed information. Moments like this were always fun on the technical side and front end of the operations, but when it came to telling major decision makers what was happening, that was another story. It came down to this, what I was getting ready to tell the Old Man was that two countries were violating international trade agreements, and furthermore, compromising an arms embargo policy which would strain international diplomacy. Basically, the skipper's decision to publish the intel report would open up a can of worms.

Once on the bridge, I approached the captain. "Sir, I am Petty Officer Cunningham from OZ Division, and I have recent imagery that you need to be briefed on." Handing him the first image of the vessel. I began to explain, "Skipper, this is a Soviet destroyer of the Udaloy class. It departed the Russian sub base of Petropavlovsk approximately 3 days ago.

The captain then asked, "Is it trailing us?" "No sir, it is not. Two days after the Udaloy departed, a cargo ship carrying Russian manufactured weapons departed from a North Korean port, where the Udaloy picked it up yesterday. Sir, based on other collection platforms, OZ assesses that the destroyer is providing escort for the cargo carrier, purportedly en route to Iran."

The captain raised his head slowly from looking at the pictures and looked at me. He cut his eyes to the right to glance at the helmsman, who was on the helms wheel and then fixed his eyes back on me. He asked if I had the reports that would corroborate with the pictures. I said, "Yes sir" and handed them to him. Again, he cut his eyes back to the helmsman and commanded, "Helmsman, set a course for 2-1-0!" The skipper then told me, "Have Lt. Commander Johnson call me asap." As I got back into the division shop, I stuck my head into the commander's office and told him the skipper wanted the commander to call him. I went to sit at an open desk. Chief Vanknockan asked me how it went. I just put my hands on my head and told him, "The commander is going to chew me a new one. The Old Man did not have any response, he just wanted to know what we had!" About 20 minutes later, the commander yelled out my name. "Cunningham! Come in here!" I replied to the chief, "Here we go."

Once in the commander's office, I stood there waiting to be asked to be seated, but it never came. The commander asked me to provide another update to him using the large map on his wall. I went over the events of collection and provided the gist of my report to him. He in turn said, "Good! At 1900 hours you are to report to the port side at weapons bay #3 and see the boatswain's mate on duty. You are going to be a part of the log-rep with the flagship." Feeling confused and like I had really screwed up at the same time, I said "Aye, Sir." The commander looked at me and said, "You don't understand, you are going to be going over with the logistical replenishment, not to work it. You are to rep over to the Blue Ridge and brief the admiral just what you briefed me, stay overnight, and be helo'd back sometime in the next couple of days. I piped back to the commander, "Log-rep!?" He stated, "Yes, log-rep. The skipper has decided to set the ship on condition black tonight, and instead of pushing a helo out to the Blue Ridge, where it would draw attention, we are going to get you over there via log-rep. It will look like it is a ship to ship at-sea replenishment. Not only that, that Udaloy behind us has been picking up our trash for the last several hours." "Aye, Aye, Sir," I replied.

I left the commander's office and silently gave myself a pat on the back. At the same time, I was freaking out. I have never worked a log-rep before, much less been the item that is sent over! At-sea log-reps are not common and tend to be a little stressful because you need to have multiple variables synced. For starters, both ships must be traveling at the same knots. Secondly, the weather should be good, in other words, no lightening. Thirdly, the swells should be at a minimum or at least below the replenishment lines. Sending supplies over was one thing, but sending a person over was totally and altogether different. I was starting to get a little worked up. I thought a good meal at the chow deck would put things in perspective.

I showed up at the weapon's deck and told the boatswain's mate (BM) on duty who I was. He was a first class, normal height guy with very broad shoulders and had Carson written on his shirt. BM1 Carson gave me a quick run-down on what I needed to expect and walked me over to the rails to check out how the log-rep was going so far. It seemed a bit overwhelming.

The waves between the ships seemed to be overly large busting up against the ship's bulkheads, and I began to get a queasy feeling. I started chucking up what I had eaten a couple of hours before. BM1 asked if I was up to this. I told him, "I got this, it's just some little nerves." The other guys around helping with the log-rep were snickering. I recall thinking, "It figures. You know the old saying, 'what goes around comes around.'" I used to always laugh when new sailors would come aboard, and once we were underway, you would see them barfing over the side. The Marine detachments were the worst. He began to suit me up with a harness vest and showed me a few safety precautions. He and his team helped hook me up to the lines where I would be pulled over. Going over between the ships seemed a lot longer than the eight minutes it took. The waves misted me completely wet and at times gushed me. The ships rocked up and down and swayed back and forth closer together and then swayed outward. What made it worse was the operation was all at dark and the only light illuminating was the moon and green lamps from the ships' replenishment bays. After a few moments it was over and I was on board the Blue Ridge taking off my gear and checking the condition of my files.

I was met by a lieutenant, an aide to the 7th Fleet Commander, Admiral P. Miller. Admiral Miller would later become DCNO, Deputy Chief of Naval Operations. The lieutenant escorted me to the Blue Ridge's Combat Information Center (CIC) and then into a briefing room. He had me sit as he explained the proper military protocols that I needed to be aware of when addressing a naval officer above the rank of O6. I began to get a little nervous as I had never briefed at this level before. I was getting ready to tell this national level decision maker that Iran is violating arms embargoes with the Soviets. This man was on the phone every day with the Joint Chiefs of Staff, the Defense Secretary and other powers that be. I had to remind myself that my job was to stick to the facts. That was all that I was there for.

The admiral along with other senior aides came into the briefing room and immediately took their respective seats without making any eye contact. Once all the attendees were seated and comfortable, the admiral broke silence and said, "Son, what are we here for, and I understand you had a wet experience getting over here." I replied, "Yes Sir, the seas were not kind." The gentlemen all chuckled, then the Admiral said, "Welcome aboard. We thank you for making the trip. What do you have for us?" I then began my briefing.

"Admiral Miller, distinguished aides, my name is William Cunningham, an intelligence specialist on board the USS Midway. At approximately 0920 this a.m., the Midway's Snoopy Team was launched to photograph an unidentified combatant trailing five miles behind the carrier. These pictures, sir, reveal that this vessel is a Soviet destroyer of the Udaloy class. Two miles bearing 090 was a cargo ship, which we were able to also fly over to photo shoot." As the fleet commander studied the photos I continued. "Sir, based on IMINT reporting, the Udaloy departed from the sub base Petropavlovsk two days ago, on or about (OA) 1300 hours, with a heading of 1-8-0 degrees toward the Sea of Japan. Separate reporting from HUMINT indicated that the Panamanian registered cargo ship, carrying Soviet military grade arms departed from a North Korean port in the vicinity of Pangyon three days ago, one day ahead of the Udaloy reporting. Admiral, OZ on the Midway assesses that this Soviet destroyer rendezvoused with the arms carrier to provide escort and force protection as it sets for a destination to an unknown port in Iran. Based on its current speed and known weather conditions, we project this shipment will arrive in the next four to five days.

Sir, that concludes my brief, do you have any questions?" Hoping that there were going to be no questions I began closing my briefing folder. However, there's always a question. If not from the senior official, there's almost always one from the aides. Sure enough, an O6 (captain) sitting next to the admiral had to ask one. Questions from aides or assistants usually were produced to make them look good or equally important. I hated that. Nonetheless, the captain asked, "Petty Officer Cunningham, why do you think these Soviet arms are destined for Iran and not some other region?"

With a thoughtful pause I concluded by saying, "Sir, the Soviets in Afghanistan are currently evacuating. Iraq has been in a conflict with Iran on the border for some time now, and frankly has been compliant to the NATO arms embargo. Iran, however, has not. Furthermore, this arms carrier has been previously reported entering into Iranian ports." I stood by and waited for another question. The admiral commented, "Thank you son, has ONI been notified?" I replied, "Yes Sir, a draft MIR went out about three hours ago." "Good job son," the admiral stated. "The LT will show you where you can grab something to eat and bed down."

As we made our way to the berthing area, I noticed the ship was immaculate. It appeared that the bulkheads were freshly painted and the overhead clean and wiped down. After all, it was the flagship. The food was better and the berthing seemed roomier. As we walked down the passageway I was glad to be done with the day. We had days like this, but they never came at this level of high interest.

27

Where I Belong

Chapter 2

SECRET AGENT MAN

Growing up I used to watch a show called *Secret Agent Man*. I dreamed of being one of those cold war spies traveling around the world conducting cloak and dagger operations. I suppose this was as close as I was going to get, being a part of the Naval Intelligence Community. At the time, there were only 2,300 of us in the Navy that could do what we did. We were spread across the fleet on carriers, small boys, SEAL teams and intelligence agencies and embassies around the world. We had to be experts at Soviet arms recognition, from Alpha fast attack subs to Typhoon ballistic missile nuclear subs. We had to understand the variants of Soviet bombers to fighter aircraft as in Bears, Badgers and Bisons to Fulcrums and Flankers. We not only had to memorize the air and maritime order of battle, but equally know the ground order of battle from tanks, surface to air missiles, to shoulder launch RPGs. Additionally, we had to learn ranges, displacements, capabilities and other associated weapons systems. We were trained to know all the Soviet bases, what their inventory was and, if we were good, we would know where they were selling their equipment.

The US Navy was relentless at training us. Our schools were the second hardest schools in the world, next to the Navy's Nuclear Engineering Sub training. Students that flunked out of Nuke training would end up in the Intel schools. The US Navy would spend an average of $125,000 to $200,000 on each intel specialist in the navy, not to mention the cost of insuring we were cleared with top secret clearances with numerous sensitive compartmented information (SCI) caveats behind our cleared credentials. We were trained as operational intelligence specialists on the sea and as human intelligence specialists assisting other governmental agencies (OGA) as well as embassies across the world. Some of us also had advanced training by the Air Force for imagery intelligence, which was a highly coveted skill-set during the cold war. Again, another long school with a massive amount of data to absorb and memorize. I knew more about the Soviet Navy and their military infrastructure than our own.

Becoming an intelligence specialist was no easy matter. If you did not sign up for it when you entered the Navy, you could pretty much guess that you were not going to get into the community unless you retested and re-enlisted and had a letter stating you were eligible. My pathway was different. I actually began in engineering as a machinist mate. I went to the fireman's basic engineering school and then to the fleet where I was assigned a steam room. I hated it as my schedule was 4 on 8 off and so on. The average temperature in steam room # 4 was 120 degrees. My typical responsibilities were to monitor the steam condensers and centrifugal pumps.

Instead of building my engineering career, I decided to ask if I could volunteer my time in OZ when I had time off to get on the job training to see if I would like the work. After about two months I was hooked and began to file all the needed paperwork to change my rate from machinist mate to intelligence specialist (IS). They call this "striking out." It was a long process and went through numerous red-tapes and personnel decision makers. Once approved, I would be assigned a basic intel school and would have to commit to coming back to the ship as an IS.

The navy career change for me was important. As mentioned before, I always wanted to be a "Secret Agent Man." Now I was one. Flying all over international waters, secretly monitoring and collecting data on our enemy and finding new hostiles to report on, not to mention connecting pieces of the world's global puzzle together to brief high level decision makers on ultra-sensitive matters with regard to our national security. Some might think that this was all in a day's work for us guys in the intel world and in one sense they are right. On the other hand, there are many, dare I say most, who do not know what it takes to keep a nation secure. Therefore, I felt good about my assessment and brief to the 7th Fleet Commander.

As the evening drew closer, I found an open rack in the berthing compartment where the lieutenant assigned me. I was able to get a nice shower and lay down for a night's rest. While pondering on the day's events and re-thinking everything I fell asleep. Sleeping was always a problem for me as I had a difficult childhood which triggered some unmentionable issues in my life. Sleep always resulted in me waking up, rocking back and forth, and wrestling with some depression that I often masked, yet struggled with.

As I fell asleep, I began to dream about some uncomfortable home memories. My mom was a nurse's assistant and my dad a mechanic. They both had drinking problems. One night my mother came home early and decided to unwind. She made us kids some rice and chicken and then put on a record to play on the turn-table that belonged to my dad. She poured herself a glass of wine and began to dance around a little and we kids joined in. It was blissful moment. Then my dad came home. He started yelling at her, "Why are you playing my stereo?" She grabbed him a beer, handing it to him and she answered back, "Its ours." He slapped the beer out of her hands, pushed her to the floor, and yelled back at her, "Don't ever mess with my stuff, woman!" He kept yelling and ranting. She got up and began to fight back, but he hit her again and again. He went over to the closet, grabbed a baseball bat, and went over to the stereo and began hitting it, breaking it up into pieces. My twin brother and little sister ran into the bedroom and climbed underneath the bed to hide. I ran behind the hallway door where I could see what was going on through the hinge opening. I stood there watching my beaten mother and hearing my bat-wielding dad yell throughout the house threatening to find us kids to beat too.

Standing behind that door, fear welled up inside me and I began to cry, holding back any sound that would come out of my mouth. I just let the stream of tears flow down my seven-year-old face. Hearing him stomp around the house and seeing my mother lying beaten on the floor, culminated such fear in me that I messed myself in my footy pajamas. I was too scared to move out from behind that door. As I watched him stomp out of the living room past the hallway door into the dining room and then the kitchen, I was suddenly grabbed by my collar and jerked out from behind the door. My oldest sister placed her hand over my mouth so I would not make a peep. She rushed us three little kids past my mother lying on the floor unconscious, out the front door, down the steps, and behind a driveway retaining wall. We looked back into the house and saw my dad yelling and whirling his bat around through the windows. My sister turned to me and anxiously whispered, "Chuck, run down to the neighbor's and tell them to call the cops. Tell them everything that has happened, and hurry!" With tears still in my eyes I took off running down the street with my soiled pj's on, crying louder and louder. Then...

I abruptly awoke breathing so hard that I felt like I could not catch my breath. This was something that I struggled with off and on throughout my life. I would get up for an hour or two and pace back and forth thinking of those horrible memories. I would just try to work through it until I tired myself back to sleep.

This time however, I stayed up. It was 0330 a.m., so I went to the catwalk to check out the water and shake off my demons. As I looked over the ocean and, on the horizon, I saw a landscape of lights. Based on where we were, I figured we were heading into Subic Bay, Philippines. Once we got into Subic, I grabbed my gear and headed out to locate where my ship was moored. Subic Bay was a favorite port of the sailors. It was, for all intents and purposes, a sailor's port. I suppose one could call it the Las Vegas of the Pacific Rim. The weather was always near a perfect 81 degrees. It was tropical and cheap. The girls were beautiful, and food was always tasty. However, it was still a poverty stricken third world city.

After locating my ship and changing my clothes, I went to check in with Commander Johnson in OZ to give him a follow-up report of my briefing to the task force commander. It was just a quick update as I knew that messages were going back and forth already. I also insured that I had permission to enjoy the port call. We had been at sea for several days and although short, I was looking forward to getting off the iron carrier. The commander told me that we all had a 48-hour pass. Port calls were good and bad. For the most part, good for morale, but bad because most of the time, us sailors would not sleep until we got in every minute of our R&R. After spending time on the ship, one learns that it is best to take advantage of every hour off the ship that one can handle. Once you are back on the ship and underway you may not see land for another two or three months. There were many times we had scheduled port calls but were diverted to provide force protection by staging ourselves a couple of hundred miles off the coast of some country experiencing some international or trans-regional conflict.

Port calls were also bad in the sense that we normally did not know how to behave ourselves when we were left to our own devices. Leaving the ship and walking toward the check point out into the local economy was never a pleasant stroll. We had to cross a bridge over a river we called "shit river" because many of the make-shift houses and businesses along the river used it to channel their sewage. It always smelled. Walking across the bridge was a sight you would never forget. You would not only have to deal with the putrid smell, but equally look in shock at all the kids playing around in the water. It literally was a cesspool and there were always locals scattered down in the river. Once across the bridge, the town of Subic Bay had a one-lane road running up the street which was packed with cars and colorful three-wheeled jeepies with religious ornaments and bells around the canopy. Literally hundreds of locals and sailors populated the streets, shops, and bars. To say the least, it was always crowded to the point you would easily shoulder bump someone walking about. Most of the bars where either run by a local family or ex-patriots. They would consist of former US or UK armed forces personnel who had visited the ports before and loved the life and cheap cost of living, so they moved there to have their own business. They basically checked out of the western culture altogether. An ex-pat could live like a king for about $12,000 a year. That amount could buy them a house on the beach or near the beach, a live-in maid, and a girlfriend to boot. Owning a bar was a plus. Many of these guys would work for about three months as a security professional or protection security detail (PSD) for some defense or oil company in another country and then back to the Philippine Islands (PI).

The bars and diners were always blaring loud music and came with a bunch of go-go girls. If you have ever heard the term "girl in every port" with regard to sailors, this is where they got it. The bars were always flooded with girls. Most of the time they would be working for the bars picking up sailors coming in for some San Miguel beer. They gave a portion of what they made back to the bar owner. These go-go girls would wear heavy perfume and tight shorts. They'd get real close to you, blatantly asking, "Hey, you want good time?" Sailors would then ask, "How much?"

33

It is an interesting transaction to witness. I recall sitting at the bar next to a guy getting his thighs or back rubbed by one of the go-go girls and dialoging over how much it was going to cost for this sailor to get his way with her. A girl would be willing to turn tricks for less than 20 bucks. Once the pesos were agreed upon, the sailor would finish up his beer or beers, joke around with his buddies and then head off to a nearby room which he would rent for 5 bucks.

The intel guys were held at a higher standard. We were not allowed to get involved with local girls due to getting caught up in a "honey-pot" situation, which is when a girl seduces a guy to solicit information out of him. She would then either sell the information or use it against him. This did not mean the intel guys didn't partake of the lovely ladies of the PI. On the contrary, the intel guys were often the worst culprits. They just could not get caught. We had about 20 guys in our division. There are a few that really stick out. Elf was the nickname of one of the guys, who was a self-proclaimed warlock. He was short and always ended up with pregnant girls. I asked him once why. He said, "Because, they can't get pregnant." Another co-worker of mine, Stimey, would later be brought up on charges for harassment. The point is, port calls were often more difficult to deal with than being at sea for extended periods of time.

My first visit to this port cured me of an indiscretion that I entertained. A year or so earlier, while I was engaged to a great girl back in NC, we pulled into Subic Bay for a port call. I had collected all the stories from the guys of the wild times that you can have in the PI. Once off the ship and heading into town to "live it up" with my buddies, I remember gasping in shock at the kids playing in the river as I crossed the bridge. We hit a couple of bars down the street on the right side to get loaded. I had a few beers and was feeling the buzz of intoxication coming on. Like all the other sailors, I was flirting around with a couple of go-go girls and was just not ready to jump into the sack with one of these local ladies yet. I knew the concerns our commander had, guarding against "honey-pots" and I also wrestled in my mind how I could justify cheating on my fiancé back at home. Part of me kept thinking she'll never find out and the other part of me knew it was morally wrong. Furthermore, I had been reading a book she had given me about Christianity. I was not a Christian, but I did believe in God.

Still struggling with lust and desire, I decided I would shake off the girls I was flirting with and make my way over to the other side of the street to get something more to eat and drink and see if I could pick out the right girl for me. I begged one of my buddies to go with me. After much reluctance and a promised meal and beer, he came along. I wobbled my drunk self over, maneuvering through people and the jeepies on the streets and sat down at the local diner and ordered another beer and a Lum Burger. While sitting there drinking my beer, getting more drunk, my speech began to slur and my vision became more blurred. I tried to control it and just relax by looking out in the streets from the diner's window. I began to stare at a jeepie directly pulled in front of the eatery. I was attempting to count the different lights on the vehicle in an effort to prove I had control from my state of drunkenness. Without notice, the jeepie pulled out and sped off. What I saw next has not only haunted me for over 25 years, but equally cured my lustful desires of having a "girl in every port" and more importantly kept me from cheating on my gal back at home.

Walking across the street from behind the jeepie was a young girl of 14 to 16 years of age. She was dressed in shorts and carrying a newspaper in her arms. As she made her way closer to the diner, she was in a perfect distance diagonal from my window where I could watch her. She was very thin with skinny arms and legs. I noticed she unfolded the rolled-up paper in her arms, lifted her shirt and placed it against her breast. Bewildered, I wiped my eyes and focused on what she was doing and noticed the newspaper in her arms was moving, then a little brown leg came out. Intently staring at her feeding this baby, I became acutely aware of the circumstances around this small city. She was trying to chat with some of the servicemen walking by, hoping to turn a trick. I was so mesmerized and shocked by what I saw, that I hadn't noticed that my burger had been brought to me and that my friend was trying to engage me in a conversation. I half-heartedly made an attempt to chat with him, but kept redirecting my attention on this little girl and her tiny baby wrapped up in a newspaper.

For some reason, I was flashing back and forth in my mind between a childhood memory and watching this girl. It was another haunted memory of seeing my mother abused. One night, when I was very young, I kept hearing a bunch of noise in the next room. I heard voices. Laughing at times and some yelling and then talking. I got concerned and climbed out of my bunk bed. I went down the hall to the door and slowly cracked it open. I saw my drunk parents half clothed, mother just in panties and father still with his pants on. I then spoke up, "Mom, are you ok?" Both of them were shocked that I was there. My mother yelled at me to go back to bed and my dad threw his shirt at me, yelling at me, "Get out of here!" while he had a tight grip on mom. I immediately ran down the hall and hid behind the door consumed by fear, as I didn't know what was going on. Suddenly, I heard their door slam and the laughing and talking continued. After snapping out of that memory, I focused back on the girl in the street in front of our window.

I then heard, "So, are you ready to have some fun tonight and get a couple of girls?" I looked at my buddy and said "Yeah, I am, and I think I got one picked out right here." I told him to hold fast, that I would be back in a minute. I got up and walked out the door to that girl on the streets. She stood up with her baby in the newspaper. I reached in my wallet and pulled out all the converted pesos I had and told her, "No boys tonight." She looked at me, took the money and said, "You want good time?" I replied emphatically, "No! No good time tonight! You go home. Take pesos and go home!" After a little more dialog, she turned around and walked back across the street and down the road. I went back inside and sat down again with my buddy to finish eating my burger and drink my beer. He looked at me and said "What in the hell was that all about?" I told him exactly what I was seeing with this little girl and her baby. I tried to explain to him that I was watching some 14-year-old girl carry a baby around, wrapped up in a newspaper, and she's out trying to turn tricks to us sailors. She probably got knocked up by one of the sailors from an earlier port call and now she's just trying to stay in the game and make money to feed herself and maybe some other family members. "When you think about it man, it's disgusting and morally wrong!" He said, "Relax man!" I then told him, "That's my girl for tonight and for every other port call we make. She got paid 60 or 70 bucks worth of pesos and doesn't have to be treated like a dog." He chuckled at me and said, "Good on you man, but not me, I plan to score big

time." I shook my head and said, "Whatever. Now pop for this meal, 'cause
I am busted."

Where I Belong

Chapter 3

PATCHING THE PAIN

The 1MC blasted the whistling sound followed by the nightly announcement, "Taps, taps, lights out! All hands turn into your bunks! Maintain silence about the decks! The smoking lamp is out in all berthing spaces." The berthing compartment was busy with sailors putting souvenirs and clothes in their storage lockers, including me. Some sailors were coming out of showers and others were just chatting about their adventures in the Subic Bay port call. The ship was pulling out in a couple of hours to regain her heading to the Indian Ocean.

As I was climbing into my rack, Petty Officer Dave came around the bunks. "Cunningham, the commander wants to see you ASAP!" I replied with the question, "Why?" He said, "I don't know." I got dressed and headed back down to OZ and reported to the lieutenant commander's office. I found him reading through intel reports while flicking his highlighter up and down as he read. "Commander, you wanted to see me?" He asked me to come into his cubicle and pull the privacy screen closed as he wanted to chat with me about something.

"IS3 Cunningham, you are one of my star sailors. Although you are not as senior ranking as some of the other sailors, you do carry your weight around here." He continued, "I have been evaluating your performance and how you get along with others and you seem to have something that many of them don't have, character." I took a moment to thank him, and he began to tell me why I was in his office. He told me that I didn't seem to be one that runs with the crowd. He began to tell me about how the Navy set up an Anti-Terrorism Ops center after the Beirut bombings which occurred three years prior. He also told me about the

Navy's new initiative to embed special agents of the Naval Investigative Services (NIS) aboard ships to help with physical and classified security. Months earlier, Jonathan Pollard, a navy intelligence analyst working for ONI was captured, tried and found guilty of espionage, for stealing and selling classified documents, and handing them over to Israeli intelligence operatives. He ended up receiving a life sentence.

As the commander continued to talk, I began to wonder where this was going. He told me that the ship had a detachment of two agents on board and they needed some honest eyes and ears, so the lead agent asked him to ask who he knew that he could trust to help them. "I could only think of one person in my entire division, you!" he said. I in turn stated to the commander, "Sir, I appreciate the compliment, but what do you need me to do?" He began to tell me that the NIS detachment desired, if I was willing, to use me on a case by case basis to inform them of unusual activity from other sailors, including our intelligence team. I sat there, somewhat bewildered, almost numb to what I was hearing. I then spoke up and said, "Sir, are you asking me to be an informant?" He leaned back in his chair and looked at me for a few seconds with a serious look in his eyes and said, "Cunningham, I have no one else that I would choose. You are it!"

I felt honored and frightened at the same time. Being a trained analyst was not a problem. I liked trying to figure out things and didn't mind working hard at it. However, being an informant on a ship that is out to sea in a confined space with a bunch of guys that were already paranoid enough was something totally different. I reluctantly leaned forward putting my face into my hands and said to myself, "William, I hope you don't regret this." I looked up at Commander Johnson and said, "Sir, I am your man!" The commander pulled several pieces of paper from his locked desk file cabinet and told me, "Your clearance will be upgraded, and you will have to fill out this paperwork to get the ball rolling. For the time being, I will authorize you to have a temporary upgrade until your final clearance comes back. This paperwork can only be filled out in my office. If someone asks why you are coming in here so much, just tell them I have tasked you to update my wall map on ship movements in our area." The commander then went over some of the paper work with me and indicated that there will be information that I may have access to on a need-to-know basis, and that I will not be allowed to mention or disclose any revelation of operations for 72 years. After reading the disclosure forms and signing them I asked, "What's next commander?"

The commander turned around in his chair, picked up the phone, and placed a call. He had a short-encrypted discussion with the person on the other end. He basically said, "I have someone that you have been needing, when do you want to see him?" He hung up the phone and turned his chair toward me and said, "Petty Officer Cunningham, I need you to report down to the Master of Arms shop tomorrow where they will escort you to the NIS shop. I had to ask the commander to give me directions. I discovered it was at the bottom of the ship in a place I had never been before.

I then asked the commander, "What do you want me to tell the chief when I don't muster up in the morning?" He told me that he'd take care of that and for me to make my way to the NIS office after breakfast. I was dismissed and made my way back to the berthing compartment. While heading back, I began to feel paranoid that someone might have heard what the commander and I were talking about or that someone might have seen me leaving at such a late hour. I finally made it back to my rack and climbed in for some sleep, but ended up tossing and turning most of the night. I only slept here and there, worried about what was next for me.

The following morning, I sat in the mess deck eating my breakfast and looking about the area wondering if there was someone here that was violating security protocol. I pondered the fact that there were many soldiers I was looking at that I would possibly end up having to report against. As I looked about the mess deck I knew of a couple of guys that were probably going to end up on one of my reports. I did not like the idea of being a snitch. It just bothered me and I was beginning to struggle with it. As I finished eating I considered the magnitude of what I was getting myself into.

I made my way down to the bottom of the ship into voids that I didn't know existed. I came up to a small compartment and entered in to find a big guy who was a 2nd class master-at-arms (MA). He was basically one of the ship's police assets. I mentioned to him who I was and that I was there to see the agent afloat. He escorted me to an inner compartment to the special agent in charge. I told the NIS agent who I was and that Lt. Commander Johnson had tasked me to come down and see them. The agent said, "Cunningham, thank you for being here. Do you know why you are here?" I said, "Yes sir, I do. The NIS has a detachment onboard and wishes to use trusted sailors to help them with security matters." He replied, "That's right," and handed me a couple pieces of paper that were affidavits and non-disclosure forms. "IS3 Cunningham, we are asking you to sign these forms, acknowledging that you will report any and all suspicious activity, without prejudice, and that you will not ever disclose any operation details to anyone unless they have a need to know." "I understand, sir," I replied. "I thought that I already signed these forms up in the commander's office." The NIS agent said, "That was for the upgrade in your clearance. This is for working with us."

The intelligence community was often intentionally a complex beast. There may be certain agencies that were tasked with specific executive orders, but it didn't mean that these agencies would not just grow other programs out of their original tasks. One case in point, ONI started the NIS after the Beirut bombing. The FBI realized that they could not do it all alone, so it was decided that each of the armed services would create their own investigative services. The Army has the Criminal Investigative Division known as CID, the Air Force has OSI which stands for Office of Special Investigations, and the Navy has the Naval Investigative Services or NIS, (now known as NCIS - Naval Criminal Investigative Services). Each branch now has federalized officers that cover activities related to their services. Whether it be murder, rape, theft, contracting fraud or others, they will investigate according to Uniform Code of Military Justice or the UCMJ.

The agent then stated that he wanted to start me off slow. "Cunningham, there is a probability that someone, or maybe more than one, in your division is running a theft ring, stealing personal belongings from other sailors. If that is true, then there is the possibility that if these same sailors are stealing from each of you, they are likely to steal from the US Government. What we desire to do is set up a sting operation. We are going to lace a few hundred dollars with print powder and have you place it in your back pocket (make sure you have no name on your dungarees). Hang it up on a hook in your berthing area with the money partially exposed. If someone takes the money, we will be able to trace it."

I complied and was told to report to them as soon as I noticed that the money was stolen. After being handed the money in a plastic bag, I tucked it in my pants and headed back to OZ to report for the daily duties.

That night after work was complete in our division I went back to my berthing area. I had decided to wait until later when there was very little light and personnel activity in the berthing compartment. This would allow me to inconspicuously plant the money in dungarees on a hook along the pathway. It was easily noticeable if someone wanted to steal the money.

The next morning, I jumped in the shower. As I was getting dressed afterwards I heard a guy yelling for some of the others in the berthing bay. "Hey! Elf, come here and look at this! Someone has money sticking out of their jeans." I was around the other side and could hear them talking. Then louder, "Hey! This money is laced with tracing powder! Someone is trying to set us up!!" I immediately popped my head around the corner as if I was just as concerned. Frankly, I was! I was concerned that I would be found out as the OZ snitch. I told Daniels, "Dude, you are right," as I grabbed the bills. "It does look like something fishy is going on here." I told Daniels and Elf that I would take the pants and money down to the commander and they should go with me. We would tell him that we found all this and wanted to turn it in to him, letting us off the hook of any suspicion anyone had of us. So that is exactly what we did.

My heart was pounding! All I could think about is how I was going to explain this and still make myself look credible to the commander and to the guys who were believed to be shady. After entering the commander's office, I allowed Daniels to talk and I followed his lead. The commander then acted surprised and stated that he was going to look into it then dismissed us. Daniels, Elf and I went into our work area and found a place to work. Each of us seemed to be quiet. I thought it might be that each of us was wondering about each other and the situation. I finally concluded that they didn't think I could ever be a snitch as I kind of played it down saying that it wasn't a cool thing to do to your friends. Later in the day, I went back to the commander to update mapping the board. He approached closely and whispered, "Cunningham, we will try something different later." I was relieved to know that he wasn't overly disappointed.

A few days later I met up with the NIS agent. He instructed me that he desired to let this die out and we would resume again with another scenario. He also told me that he was covered up with other pressing issues. One being a sabotage on the ship by an unknown person. Someone was starting fires in the voids. This was a huge issue. Safety was paramount on the ship. The Navy had had a series of mishaps on other ships and didn't need this for their safety rating. Furthermore, it jeopardized the welfare of over 3,500 sailors. It would only take one fire to get out of control and hit a JP5 fuel line. A few hours later I heard the captain come on the 1MC intercom stating, "Hear ye, hear ye all hands. This is the captain. I have a message that I need each of you to clearly hear me on. We have had a series of fires on board and believe it is due to a person trying to sabotage the ship putting all the sailors in harm's way. If you catch this weakling or know who it is, you are to bring him up to my bridge immediately. And by the way, there are a lot of steel ladder wells up to my bridge and accidents are known to happen on the way up." He then made a few short comments about safety and praised us men about the good work we were doing.

There was another incident that I was discussing with the NIS agent. They were watching someone in the weapons division. There were reports that this person was wanting to steal armaments and either sell them or get them off the ship. Later, I found out that they caught someone with a war-head that he had unmounted from the fuselage and hidden in his bunk area. I thought it was a bit far-fetched, but when we pulled back into port a couple of months later, there were three black cars waiting on the pier. They escorted this guy off the ship first and took him away. We never heard any more of the incident. It was kept quiet due to what and who was involved.

Security was at an all-time high with the Navy. We were still feeling the ramifications of the USS Stark being shot at with two Exocet French missiles by an Iraqi fighter plane for no reason. Thirty-seven sailors died as a result. The Iraqi government claimed that they had executed the pilot, but later we found out they didn't. Numerous ships were positioning themselves along the mouth of Hormuz canal acting as an envoy to escort Kuwaiti tankers which were being attacked by Iranian mines on the way

44

into Kuwait. The US maneuvered Navy assets along with two SEAL platoons to support what later became known as Operation Ernest Will (OEW). Iran and Iraq had been at war for eight years and this was one of Iran's economic terrorist tactics to hinder free trade agreements. Following the attack on the USS Stark, and the implementing of OEW, the United States also initiated another secret operation called Operation Praying Mantis. US assets would attack Iranian mining ships as a retaliation effort from a previous mining attack on the USS Sam Roberts. The success of these naval operations hinged on our fleet's guidance and direction. I was part of the 7th Fleet, which worked with USCENTCOM to deter heightened activity in the Middle East. As a result of these operations the Iranians were pressured to agree to a cease fire agreement with Iraq, ending this eight-year war. Nonetheless, the entire Navy was on guard for various reasons, whether it be security violations, naval combatant operations, safety issues, or intelligence mishaps. The tension trickled downhill and we all felt it.

While there were several other operations I was involved in, I lessened my role with the NIS detachment due to an interest in training for a new career as an explosive ordinance disposal (EOD) diver. Over the past year, being involved in some form or fashion with these operations, the Navy was recruiting heavily for EOD divers. I had researched it and decided that I was going to boost my intelligence career by being the only intel sailor qualified EOD specialist and Navy diver. The Navy had a very similar training program for divers like they did for the SEALs. It was considered a shorter version of the BUDS Navy SEALs training.

I began a rigorous training plan. My daily 10k route ended with me running up a steep set of steps to the top of a small mountain. I began to hit the gym every day building muscle and strength. Jumping rope and running around the flight deck were all part of my training. I had to get in the best shape of my life. In my mind I was always trying to do better and be something more. In many regards there is nothing wrong with this kind of ambition; however, my motives were not to be something better for the sake of being good at something, but rather, I pushed myself to extremes because I was haunted by my past. I was running from it when I took on new assignments or signed up for new training, like the EOD program. It was all that I had that would ease the pain in my head and heart. I was doing whatever I could to re-invent myself because I hated my past.

Much of my pain came not from seeing my mother abused, but rather from memories of when my mother had enough and decided to get a divorce from my father and put all of us kids in a children's home. It is a memory that I just can't get out of my mind. All six of us brothers and sisters were taken to the Carolina Children's Home in Columbia, SC. The campus was very clean with about eight large houses and one chow hall. Each of us kids were divided in each of these houses per our age group and gender. The boys on one side of the campus and the girls on the other. My mother came by each house to tell us goodbye and let us know that we were going to be okay. I remember when she came to our house. My twin brother and I were standing outside on the sidewalk giving her a hug and saying our goodbyes. I really was unsure what was going on at the age of eight but knew that it was not good. We had been in an abusive, alcoholic home for years. We had stayed with my grandparents off and on during many of the unstable moments and now this was just another thing we were to deal with.

She leaned over and gave my brother a kiss and a hug and then came to me. I just kissed her and threw my arms around her neck and started crying, "don't leave us here!" She repeatedly told me that we were going to be okay and that she would see us soon. She then got in her car and drove off. As my brother and I stood there watching the car drive further and further away, he said, "She's not coming back." I looked at him with tears in my eyes and began to run after the car, crying, "Come back! Come back!"

I got about 20 feet from where I was standing when the car disappeared. I stopped, turned around and just looked at my brother and cried. I walked back to him, reached out to grab his hand, and I said, "Let's go inside." The house mother, Miss Elliot was a large, elderly lady. She tried to assure us that we were going to be alright. The house we lived in was filled with boys 8 to 12 years of age. There were about ten of us living there. I did not know what was going on at the time, just that I was separated from my older brother and sisters, and that my mom left us in a home with strangers. I felt lonely and abandoned, confused and hopeless. I only got to see my siblings when we went to chow hall.

We would be there for several years getting weekend visits with her. She would later remarry and get us out of the children's home, but within six or seven months she struggled with alcoholism and prescription drug addiction. She and my stepdad put us back in the children's home for another year. It is something that I never wanted to relive, so I poured my life into other things to help me cope with those years. The EOD thing was just another patch for the pain.

Where I Belong

Chapter 4

MAKING COMMITMENTS

We had been at sea for several months secretly supporting Operation Ernest Will and providing ad hoc air superiority if needed. We had a squadron of F-18 Hornets on board to conduct strike operations to allied countries. Due to our rapid mobile infrastructure we could have a bird launched and on-site as far as 300 miles away within 20 to 30 minutes if given the green light. Our entire purpose was to be a contingency element if the need arose. In many instances our carrier battle group could anchor itself off the coast of a continent, like Africa, about 200+ miles away in international waters. Our mere presence would keep any ongoing conflicts at a minimum. This would often allow the leaders in Washington to either negotiate or work on diplomatic issues within the region.

The word came down from the Chief of Naval Operations that we were going to be relieved by another carrier and that we were to make our way with an east heading to provide security operations for the 1988 Olympics. North Korea was still at war with South Korea. The United States had several hundred thousand US military personnel stationed in the south to provide force protection to our allies. Our main objective was to provide security along the 38th parallel, a dividing line which separated North Korea with its communist ideology and South Korea with its evolving democratic processes. Interestingly enough, in 1988, there were still two major super powers that were under communist regime that would be attending the summer games, the former USSR (Soviets) and East Germany. The US and other participating countries had lingering fears from the 1972 Munich Massacre when West Germany was hosting the Olympics. In Munich, several Palestinian members of the terrorist group Black

September, kidnapped and murdered 11 Israeli athletes and coaches. Most of the terrorists fled in exile after the attacks. Following, the Israeli Mossad and operatives with the IDF would hunt and track down these terrorists and have them killed. This was known as Operation Wrath of God. Afterwards, there was always a need for security awareness at the Olympics. Therefore, we made our way back eastward to conduct our new assignment at the Seoul Olympics.

The entire ship's morale was boosted and on overload. To put icing on the cake some of us intel guys were going to be assigned as part of a task force to collect and report information at the Olympics. Needless to say we were overjoyed with an actual shore assignment. We had been at sea for several months making circles in the Indian Ocean (IO). We were conducting endless flight ops and tracking other foes or questionable hostile merchants. I had personally been involved in daily intel briefings, writing countless intelligence reports, and sifting through thousands upon thousands of daily intelligence traffic to capture what was happening in the world. Additionally, it seemed that I was either hopping on a helo to conduct Snoopy Surveillance Operations, or running to collect information at the ships Communication Information Operations Center (CIOC), or playing NIS informant all the time. In my spare time, I would work out and train or sleep for 4 to 6 hours. At least once a week we would get a drill thrown into our schedule for us to "man our battle stations" as part of the General Quarters (GQ) exercise. This would keep us up for an extra couple of hours which affected us for the rest of the week. All the different operations combined, day and night, the GQ exercises and other training that we had to conduct along with normal work flow became very taxing on the body and soul. Day in, day out, week after week, month after month there were the same faces, same work, same food, same smell, same water, same horizon, same schedule, same conversations and so on. It became maddening at times. Everyone had their own way of coping with the stress of on-board life. The crew would find their solace in an exercise schedule, card games, on-board college classes, or going to the chapel or Bible studies. For me, I was a mixer. I mixed it up to deal with it all, but mostly I worked. I had to and often wanted to. It kept my mind busy and allowed me to prove something to myself and others as I had a pretty messed up view of myself.

Although we stayed busy we did have time on our hands that needed to be filled which could have been filled with one of the activities mentioned above, but there would always be that thorn in the flesh...that gnawing, that pondering, that many of us went through. "Why am I here and what in the world am I doing with my life?" Thoughts like this would often surface and eventually lead to the subject of faith or God. No matter how much I tried to cover or mask it by staying busy, when night came, and I was in my rack I would inevitably begin to ponder about spiritual things. It could have been the fact that I was often in potentially dangerous situations with work. It may have been any number of things, but one fact remains, I was pondering, and it was often. I learned to consider these times of pondering as sacred moments.

One particular night was no different. In just a few short days we would be setting our course heading 090 degrees directly east, as we got word that our relief carrier was inbound. I laid in my rack contemplating the new assignment and began thinking about my faith. My mind took me back to eighteen months before. It was a time that I came to a decision to turn my life over to God and believe in His plan of redemption for my life, specifically trusting that His Son, Jesus the Christ, died on a cross for my sins, wiping them away completely so that I might be forgiven and have eternal life. It was something that I came to believe in but struggled living in.

It is a vivid memory, as it is surrounded by thoughts of my marriage. The year was 1986, just one and a half years before, and I was struggling with the idea of getting married to a girl that I was dating back in North Carolina. She was eighteen at the time, and I was twenty-one. We had been in a long-distance relationship for several months. After boot camp we got engaged. I had known her since she was sixteen but didn't really pay attention to her until she was seventeen. She was young and I was young. The problem I had getting married wasn't with her, my struggle was with me. Amy was a pretty, long-haired blond. She was quiet, had beautiful green eyes and walked as if she glided on air. She was the type of person that was never in a hurry, and when she spoke it was as if she was not meant for earth but rather meant to sing heavenly praises with the rest of the angels. Although she had her own personal teenage struggles, she was a person of deep faith. As I recall, during our period of courting, she had a huge influence over me as she didn't fear being a Christian in front of me. I on the other hand, had a problem with Christianity and every other religion. I grew up in a dysfunctional, abusive home laced with divorce and then as we grew older and came out of the children's home, I saw my siblings struggle with their own relationship and substance abuse issues. I struggled because I could not make sense of why God would allow all this bad stuff to happen. Even while dating Amy I struggled with abandonment issues. I had a fear I would become abusive because of family history. More than anything, I wrestled with the fact that I was going to marry this girl and probably end up divorcing her at some point and ruining her life. Even worse, I thought that if we were able to survive and have kids, I would end up being abusive like my ol' man.

Amy would send me care packages. Her mom would make cookies and Amy would throw in a music tape she made and a letter. One package came with a book and a tape authored by a man named Keith Green. I would later find out that he was known for a "No Compromise" message in his music and writings. Many Christians had a hard time swallowing or chewing on his message. It was something I needed to hear. Keith published a book called "Last Days Collections." It was a series of writings gathered from monthly newsletters that he would send out to contributors to his ministry. His music would prick the mind and heart. After months of struggling with whether to get married and soul seeking about my own mortality I began to read this book by Keith Green. There were two chapters that really turned on the light for me. They were titled: "What's Wrong With the Gospel Pt. 1 and 2". These two chapters outlined for me everything that I saw wrong with Christianity. I learned how many Christians didn't even quote the Bible while they thought they did. He wrote about obedience and how so many people make excuses for not becoming a Christian because of how other so-called Christians believe a man-made gospel and not a biblical gospel. Keith wrote about what it takes to follow Christ - complete abandonment of self and complete trust in Christ's work of atonement. The more I read his message about the problems with the gospel, the more I agreed. I began reading it with the mind-set of, "Finally, a guy who is getting it right, putting Christians in their place as hypocrites." The more I read the more I was agreeing with Keith. What I didn't realize was that Keith was teaching me what it meant to be a Christian. Keith ended the Bible study with a written exhortation: *"Beloved family, the world around us is going to hell. Not because of communism, not because of television, not because of drugs, or sex, or alcohol, or the devil himself.* **It is because of the Church! We are to blame!** *We alone have the commission, the power, and the truth of God at our constant disposal to deliver sinner after sinner from eternal death. And even though some are willing to go... into the streets, the prisons, foreign lands, or even next door, they are taking a watered-down, distorted version of God's message which He has not promised to anoint. That is why we are* **failing.** *And unless we admit that we are failing, then I'm afraid there is no hope for us or the world around us. We have the choice between causing eternal tragedy for our whole generation, or bringing our beloved God a whole family full of "good and faithful servants."*

I laid there after reading these series of articles. With tears beginning to fill my eyes I began to pray. I didn't know what to say or how to say it, but I just began to talk to God about all my struggles. All of them - hating my father for the physical abuse that went on in our home, the abandonment of being placed in a children's home, the abuse and guilt that I experienced while there. I talked to God for a long time, discussing my issues of living in a messed-up world and concern for my future and getting married. I told God how I didn't want to get married and could not see how it would work out due to all my baggage, all my guilt, and all my burdens of feeling like a man of failure. I remember talking to God about how I was born into it and I was destined for the same path. Then, as I discussed these things with God, I clearly heard Him speak to me in my mind. It was as if He interrupted me to remind me of the most important fact that I had left out in my chat with Him. Lying there, with tears filling my eyes and beginning to run down the side of my face, dripping onto my pillow, I heard God speak to me. He said, "William, the problem with all your issues, your abuse, guilt and fear of marriage is my son, Jesus Christ." God began to speak to me and tell me that every issue I had in life, my darkest problems stemmed from an absence of Jesus in my life and circumstances. As I lay in my bunk with other sailors around me in the berthing compartment, tears flooded down my face. I tried to muffle the groans as I told God that I didn't think I could marry this girl because of my abusive baggage. God then told me, "Yes you can! Jesus has to be your foundation and the Bible has to be your blueprint to build and maintain your marriage." He then told me that I needed to write a letter to my dad and let him know that I have been forgiven, I am a Christian, and that I also forgive him.

I then prayed, "God if this is all real, and you are speaking to me and Jesus can change my life, then I want to trust you with my life." I asked Him to forgive me of my hatred of my father and family situation and my fear of commitment. Then I said, "I don't know how to do this God or what I am supposed to say, but I desire you to come in my life and change me from the inside out." After I prayed that prayer I rolled over and put my face into my pillow and cried more. It was as if I was a wild horse and my will had finally been broken. I was not sure what exactly was taking place, but I did know that something was.

The next day I wrote my fiancé a letter to tell her about my experience and decision. I was excited and yet scared at the same time. I wasn't sure how she was going to take it or if she would believe the same as I did. I knew she was a Christian, but I just didn't know to what extent. I knew that she loved me. I had experienced that first hand before I left to join the Navy. I had driven up from Columbia, SC where I was living with my sister at the time and working for my grandfather in one of his hardware stores. It was something I had been doing for several months because of our long-distance relationship. We went out for a pizza and movie and drove back to her house. I stopped at the bottom of the mountain she lived on and placed the car in park. I just wanted to talk. I began to tell Amy that I had joined the Navy and that I wasn't going to be around much and thought I should just be honest and tell her. She was a little taken back by my statement but put her hand on my arm and gently said, "That's ok. I will wait." I said, "You don't understand. I am leaving, and I don't know when I will be back again. I have requested to be sent as far away from here as I can." Again, in her gentle and stable voice, she said, "Ok, then I will wait." Feeling a little unaccomplished at this point of not getting my message across to this girl, I finally told her that I was going to sail the seven seas and live the life of a sailor. It would probably be in both of our best interests to consider dating other people as I was going to be gone for three or four years and don't think it would be fair to her. She again placed her hand gently on my arm, slightly squeezed it, and looked dead in my eyes and said to me, "William, you don't understand. I love you and I will wait!" Something clicked in me at that moment. It was as if a wall had been torn down and I could finally see the other side of something beautiful. I was so touched that she kept telling me that she'd wait that it turned on a light for me. For the first time in my life, I felt that I didn't need to push someone away and that someone loved me and wasn't going to abandon me. For the first time ever, I was getting a glimmer of what real love was.

Where I Belong

Chapter 5

PORT CALLS

A couple of weeks had gone by as we left the Arabian Sea and made our way to Korea. We had three port calls scheduled. The first was to be the east African port named Mombasa, Kenya, located below Mogadishu, Somalia on the Indian Ocean. I believe our two day stop over there was purely diplomatic. Just a couple of months before their general elections were taking place and for the first time in the government's history, they were revising how they conducted the election processes. In the new process, the party leaders would stand behind presidential candidates. This was a problem in that there was only one political party in Kenya which had about 500,000 members. Anyone else that would run against the current incumbent who had been in office for 15 years as president and 20 years as a vice president, would at best get a few votes, but never win. The NY Times picked up on this and published an article using indigenous sources, causing some uncomfortable diplomacy. We were tasked to make a port call and have our battle commander make a diplomatic visit while we intel spooks conducted a population assessment of the general public. It was generally a Q & A format to the public. This later became very popular with US Special Forces elements and was known as Cultural Engagement. Our next stop was scheduled for a port call in Pattaya, Thailand.

After surrendering my life to Christ just a year and a half before, I struggled with my identity as a sailor and a new believing Christian. I had tried out the chapel services a few times, but mostly tried to read the new study Bible I bought and pray. I often wrote my wife with questions and to tell her what I was going through, and she would do her best to answer based on her level of growth. I knew that something was going on within me. I could sense it but could not put my finger on it. Pattaya was a morale port call from our long deployment. It was the port call that all the guys were waiting for. Stories of wild clubs, girls and sex shows were filtering throughout the ship. All of us, including me, were being driven in our minds by carnal thoughts of unbridled pleasures. I wrestled with being Christian and living in a world that says, "Anything goes." Something that was speaking to me was a string of reports that were filtering through our division on a new disease called AIDS. In previous months, one USS Midway sailor stepped off the ship on a scheduled port call in the Philippines to see his Filipino wife whom he had met and married on a previous port call. Once he reunited with her she told him that she had AIDS and he needed to get checked out. This became a reactionary issue for chaplains, medical personnel, and the leadership as they tried to insist sailors have condoms while on liberty. It got to the point that they would even send boxes of condoms to all the departments to hand out. I recall thinking it was an odd thing, almost as if they were promoting sex.

Once we arrived we anchored off the beach about 500 yards or so from the shoreline. This was to be a three or four-day port call. We were finally able to get off the ship around 2 p.m. A bunch of us climbed aboard a water taxi to hit the strip to grab a beer and enjoy our liberty. Pattaya was exotic. Warm white beaches, lots of jet skis and other water craft. Street vendors selling all kinds of foods. We walked down the street gawking at the pretty girls and buying crunchy, fried grasshoppers. Bars were filled with women and the smell of cigarette smoke, cheap perfume, greasy food, and booze permeated each bar. Girls would walk up and flirt with us sailors while we were getting a beer, asking if we wanted a good time. Many of the guys that were married took off their wedding bands.

As the drinking got out of hand, so did the mind. We would end up trying several bars, checking out the girls before landing in one with erotic strip shows that kept us busy. At the time, I was hanging out with Stimey and Elf and we heard about another bar that was putting on a live sex show down on the far east end of the strip. We chugged our beers and headed down. While walking past the different bars and shops, sailors and girls were all over each other, loud music was projecting out of bars and beautiful girls were outside doors luring guys in with special prices on drinks and lots of girls. As we made it down to the bar with the show, we thought we would stop at the jewelry shop next to it and check out the different rings and bracelets. I wanted to get something for my wife back at home. We soon left the jewelry shop and turned the corner to go into the bar. I was immediately convicted and stunned at what I saw next. It was a girl outside the bar entrance dancing topless with only a bikini bottom on. As I stood there watching her, Stimey and Elf were making their way in and turned around to see where I was. Elf yelled over the loud music at me, "Come on Cunningham!" I looked at him and shook my head and waved for him to come back to me. When he approached, I looked at him and said, "Elf, I can't do this, do you see this girl dancing here, she is probably only 13 or 15 years old!" He chuckled and said, "So! Let's go in and have some fun." I told him again, "This isn't for me, man! I am married and I think I am just going to go back over next door and pick out some jewelry for my wife." He said, "Alright man! You don't know what you are missing." I told him that I would see him back at the ship later. I headed back into the jewelry shop to pick out something for my wife, Amy, but my mind was completely overshadowed by the pollution I had seen.

Once back at the ship later that night I ran into a shipmate of mine that I knew from the engineering department. He and I went to get some late-night chow (known as Mid-rats), and I wanted to tell him how corrupt I felt for indulging my mind with all the lustful events of this port call. I couldn't though because I didn't feel that he would understand my spiritual versus moral dilemmas. I didn't know what he believed. Luckily for me, he was married. He began to tell me about a great golf course with a good restaurant called the Siam Country Club. He asked if I wanted to hang out with him and another one of his buddies tomorrow, play some golf and check it out. I was more than eager to say yes as I felt it to be a redeeming outlet to the alternative of hanging out with my other buddies getting drunk and womanizing up and down the beach.

My next day was great. It was an easy-going day on a beautiful green golf course, blue skies with some puffy clouds and some perfect warm tropical weather. I had a great dinner with my engineer buddies and then caught a cab back to the beach strip where I caught the tail end of a live kickboxing match in the open air. There was a small Thailand guy, skinny, yet somewhat toned. They were looking for volunteers to fight him. A large marine stepped up for the challenge. This guy was huge with tattoos all over him. He not only looked mean, he smelled mean. He stepped into the ring and they began to go at it. The marine immediately dominated this poor tiny guy. As I was looking around I saw guys in the crowd begin to pass money back and forth, making bets on who would win. The bell rang and the next time out the marine looked like he was going to break this guy in half. Then, suddenly, the small Thai guy wriggles around and begins to do some type of mumble jumble dance. His legs were swinging around slapping this large marine silly. After several moments of this the marine was hanging on the ring ropes with blood pouring out of his nose and lip, barely able to stand on his own two feet. It was almost comical, yet it was a shame that this marine would have this event to remember his trip to Thailand.

I took a water taxi back to the ship, showered, and bedded down for the night. I was awakened around 0315 a.m. "Cunningham! Chief Vanknockan wants to see you immediately!" As I woke up, I asked, "For what?" "You have an EAM tasking ASAP!" My eyes popped open wide as they could and I shouted back, "WHAT! EAM for what?" "I don't know, he just told me to wake you and for you to get there as fast as you can."

The intel shop would compile an Emergency Action Message within 30 to 45 minutes after a major incident occurred. The EAM would be sent to a slew of agencies, but could not be immediately reported in the public until it was either investigated by a federal investigator or, if on foreign soil, an agency guy attached to the embassy. After frantically getting dressed I took off running through the berthing area curious as to what the message was going to entail. As I got to the gangway I picked up my speed, hopping over and through the numerous water tight hatches, yelling, "Gang-way! Man coming through!" Arriving at OZ, Chief Vanknockan already had my terminal set up and standing by. In those days, the terminals were monochrome, with green as the only color, and connected to a mainframe on the ship somewhere which dialed into an ARPNET dedicated line just for military called MILnet. ARPNET was originally designed by a bunch of egg-heads from the highly classified agency DARPA and later became what is known as today's internet.

The chief began to dictate comments from cable messages he had received from Bangkok:

"Subject: Service Member Murdered In Bangkok. "STOP." Then he followed with additional comments by saying, "Next line."

"1. Service member (Rank, Rate, Name) was found dead by local police force in Royal Bangkok Hotel in Bangkok, Thailand on or about (OA) 0245 (date)"

2. Death of service member is believed to be result of foul play."

3. Indigenous law enforcement comments: It is believed service member attached to USS Midway had purchased two prostitutes and invited them back to his hotel room. During sexual activity, one of the prostitutes used a razor blade to cut on and around service members extremities, he received severe fatal bleeding. Service member is believed to simultaneously choked the prostitute to death. Second prostitute took wallet and money from the service member and fled. She is yet to be found.

4. Service member's family has not been notified due to pending US investigation."

The chief and I finished off the report with some other pertinent verbiage and sent it out. Turning to the chief I said: "Chief, who was this guy and what department was he attached too?" The chief told me, and I was shocked as I knew *of* him but did not know him. My immediate follow up question to the chief was, "Who was with this guy? Usually there are other service members he had to be with. Surely this guy would not go all the way up to Bangkok on his own would he?" The chief just looked at me and then scratched his head. "I don't know, but I would suspect that he went there with others. NIS will be looking into it." It was reaching the top of the hour of 0500. I could go back to my rack and get some sleep or get some breakfast chow.

We also had one last day of liberty left and at this point I wasn't feeling like being back off the ship. All that was going through my head was that this sailor's mom and dad were going to get a phone call or a visitor from the USN or other service representative and be told that their son died while conducting "mission essential duties" while en route to the 1988 Olympics. It was always a lie. The truth was always something more than what others were told. Sometimes they would find out later.

In just three days we would stop over in Sasebo, Japan and conduct a replenishment operation before heading northwest up to Korea. While in Sasebo we sailors were once again showing our true colors. The small bars were flooded with sailors buying rounds of beers for their buddies and trying to hook up with local girls. It was interesting to watch how many sailors tried to pick up these local girls who did not know much English while the sailors struggled with Japanese. One sailor, Jimmy, a boiler-maker from engineering decided to jump up on a table and start dancing. Most guys in engineering have a rough job being down in the boiler or steam rooms. It is loud and over 120-degree temperature. So a little stress relief was often understood. Jimmy seemed to always get out of control after drinking more than he could handle. Jimmy's legs, arms, and up to his neck were covered in tattoos. He had been busted twice already for disorderly conduct which took a pay grade stripe against him. Initially he was a first class in the enlisted ranks, or E6, but after getting busted he lost a stripe and was now an E5, a second class. Here Jimmy was jigging around on the table top to the disco music along with a beer bottle in hand. He decided to impress everyone, especially the bar girls. He reportedly offered to show the girls his tattoos that led up his legs all the way to his testicles, where he had a set of dice imprinted there. One die had one dot, and the other die on the other testicle had two dots. Jimmy was a big fan of Backgammon, and I suppose the dice resembled the game Acey Duecy. So, as a drunk Jimmy was jigging around on the table with his pants down and a beer in one hand, he was pulling on his member with the other to show off his dice. Then, in walked Shore Patrol (SP). The SPs were sailors E5 and above that were given collateral duty to police the shores of ports to ensure sailors were conducting themselves in a manner that was appropriate. Jimmy was not meeting their criteria. After much arguing between Jimmy and the SPs, Jimmy was aggressively told to zip it up and come down. They were taking him back to the ship.

The SP's thought they only had a drunk problem on their hands, but they had worse. As they were waiting for Jimmy to zip it up, they took a moment to chat with the folks to find out how long he'd been up there. When they turned around to help him down, they noticed he was struggling with his zipper. He couldn't zip it up or down as he had gotten his foreskin caught in the zipper and was beginning to bleed. Jimmy, being too drunk to feel any pain and while still holding his beloved beer, was grabbed by the Shore Patrol in an effort to rescue him from hurting himself any further. They helped him, or should I say, literally carried him, out of the club, down a couple of blocks and to the landing quay where he would have a water taxi back to the ship about two hundred yards or so out. All the while, Jimmy is holding himself. Several of us followed along to the quay to see what was happening and how things were being handled. Jimmy just sat there on the water taxi holding himself while the SP's stood on either side of him looking perplexed. What made it worse is that we could see Jimmy starting to wince from the boat bouncing up and down on the chopping waves as it was trolling off.

Three days later, when we were back underway, I saw Jimmy on the mess deck and decided to sit down and find out how he was doing. He told me that they took him to sick bay where they gave him some stitches, put some ointment on him, gave him some pain killers, and sent him back to his berthing for rest. He explained that things got worse the next day as he woke up and had severe burning when he urinated. Jimmy told me that he went back down to sick bay to see the doc. After a series of tests they determined that he had contracted "The Clap" while visiting in Subic Bay or Thailand. They ended up giving him a penile catheterization, where they stuck a cleaning tube in his urinary track to help clean him out. Then they gave him a bunch of penicillin to take. He stated that he was in so much pain that he thought he would die. When the Navy doctor treated him it was the captain's protocol that he be informed of any transmitted disease on board his ship. Jimmy ended up with a visit to the Old Man. The skipper initiated an immediate "Captain's Mast," "Johnny on the spot," and Jimmy was demoted again, being busted down two more stripes and confined to the ship for the next six port calls. So, Jimmy went from an E6 to an E3 or a First-Class Petty Officer to a Seaman in a matter of a year. Along with that came hundreds of dollars of pay reduction. Jimmy just blew it off like it was no big thing. I remember thinking to myself that one decision can change the course of your life.

Chapter 6

GRASS IS NOT GREENER ON THE OTHER SIDE

The USS Midway pulled into Pusan, a South Korean port roughly two hours from Seoul. Pusan was a smoggy, crowded, smelly port that was very busy. For the OZ department it would be considered a working port-call. It meant that we could go out on liberty, but we were expected to collect, report, and disseminate any pertinent information. As mentioned before, there were a lot of concerns for terrorist activities to disrupt the Summer Olympics in Seoul. In addition to the Munich concerns from 1972, in 1987, Ok Hwa and another agent were apprehended as North Korean agents who planted a couple of bombs on flight KAL 858, killing all the passengers and the crew while it was en route to Bangkok. The agents got off at an earlier stop-over and fled. Once they realized they were being pursued, they lit up cyanide-laced cigarettes, a known North Korean elimination tactic and began to smoke them. Ok Hwa was captured before dying. Her partner died. Thus, tension between the two countries was escalated. This occurred one year prior to the Seoul Olympics. The North Korean president had also made statements to purposefully disrupt the Olympic games and cause problems with recent elections, all in hopes that teams would not attend the South Korean hosted Olympics.

The first day in port was like any other port call, running from one bar to the next or just touring around the city checking out the different shops. Clothing and tennis shoes were so cheap in Korea. Of course, everything was a knock-off. One could pick up a pair of Nikes for five bucks. It truly was a shopper's paradise. Whether you wanted mink blankets, shoes, or girls, you could get it real cheap. Still struggling inwardly as a Christian, I was faced with so many opportunities that tested my faith. Opportunities may not be the right word; trials may be a better word.

A bunch of us were ready for some Korean BBQ. We headed over to a local eatery and had a great big dinner and drank most of the evening. During our conversations one of the more experienced sailors was telling us about Green Street where you could go down and window shop for a girl. They would have a string of girls sitting on nicely decorated couches behind large windows. You could choose the one you wanted, pay the fee, and have a date for the evening. The guys were all wanting to go and began to give me grief about my so called up-right standards. I had bowed out of all the other ports' activities. They all knew I was married, yet they still thought I should be "one of the boys" by indulging myself with girls in all these ports. The heckling and the peer pressure and drinking was overwhelming. They decided that they were going to buy me a girl on Green Street, and I was going to have fun if it killed me. They were all tired of me moping around with just a few drinks with the guys and then bowing out of the fun. So we headed out to the city and down toward Green Street.

Although drunk, I kept thinking, "How am I going to get out of all this?" as I was literally being pulled along with these guys. Walking along, every last one of us not in our right mind, we eventually found ourselves looking through all the windows at the girls on Green Street. I don't remember how we got there or how long it took. The next thing I remember is Daniels calling out my name.

"Cunningham! Which one do you like?" I garbled back, "Guys, this isn't necessary. I don't know." Then someone replied, "Come on Cunningham, we are here now. Pick ya out a girl and have some fun!" I finally slurred a confession, "Guys, I never did this before. Uh, you know, pick out a hooker." The laughing and back slapping began, and Daniels said, "We'll help ya out then." I was standing in front of a window that had two girls in it, and he chose the one on the left and told the person in the window, "I want that one!" as he pointed to her. I was pushed over a few feet to the left into the doorway where Daniels was paying for this Korean prostitute's time. He grabbed her hand and led her to me. Pointing to me and said, "He's yours, treat him well!" Another slap on the back by someone and then a comment followed, "Don't do anything I wouldn't do!"

This all happened so suddenly that I couldn't remember how I got there. I found myself standing with this girl as all my buddies faded out of sight down the street.

I decided right there that I was not going to be a victim. This girl may deal with this every day, but I didn't. The thoughts of poor decisions that others made in port calls, like Jimmy, were ringing in my head. The girl with the infant in Subic Bay was haunting me, the exploited 14-year-old topless club dancer was bearing on my soul. I did not want this and did not ask for this, but at the same time I knew I did not work hard enough to stop it no matter how intoxicated I was.

What also bothered me to no end was that I was a naval intelligence professional with a high security clearance. Conduct like this, if found out by my department, would discredit me. I would be brought in for a formal inquiry, questioning me on whether I knew this girl, if I knew her background, where she was from, how long she had been tricking the streets of Seoul, and if she was a North Korean agent or not? The implications could be explosive. More than any other thought that I pondered in those few short moments was how would I live with myself as a husband to a wife I barely knew due to being overseas all the time. My new Korean friend was taking me by the hand down a hall to a room. As she opened the door, I was reaching in my back pocket for my wallet. When we entered the room, I said, "I can't do this!" and handed over cash I had pulled from my wallet. She looked at me and said, "Nee, nee. We lay together," as she pointed to the bed. I took her hand, laid the cash in her palms, and said, "No. Go home! And I go home!" I then turned around and stumbled my way out the door. As I stood in front of the Green Street Korean brothel, I looked to the left and the right down the streets and realized that I had no idea where I was. I didn't know how or where I needed to go to get back to the ship.

I turned to my right and began to walk with the intention of finding a cab to take me back to the shuttle area to catch a bus back to the ship. As I made my way down the street, beginning to feel that I had done the right thing by getting out of that situation with the Korean hooker, I was able to flag down a cab. I got in and told him where I needed to go and immediately remembered that I had handed the girl all the cash I had in my wallet. I rapidly looked back in my wallet to ensure that was the case, then started checking my pockets. I didn't have any cash. The cabby was already on his way and I had to tell him that he had to stop because I had no money. He pulled over and I stumbled out, beginning to feel queasy with anxiety. Walking down the street, the urges of alcohol sickness began to set in. I walked over to a very small median with bushes in the sidewalk area, knelt down, and attempted to fight the urge to vomit but could not hold it back. I ended up spending the next few moments emptying my gut of all its contents, heaving and heaving everything within me, until I had nothing left to heave up. I decided to just lay there to collect myself and began to think of my entire night and how happy I was that I didn't commit to the ways of my buddies. But I was soon overtaken by a great deal of guilt. I knew that just because I did not commit to laying with that prostitute, in my heart I wondered if I would enjoy it, and secretly a part of me wanted to. The moral dilemma had set in, and I was miserable. It was as if I had actually committed the act of adultery. Although my physical being was miserable, drained, tired, broken, and sick, what made me miserable was how filthy I felt in my heart and mind. There was something not right about me and I knew it.

I laid there praying out to God, asking Him to help me, forgive me, and relieve this turmoil I was in. I drifted off to sleep. Later, I awoke, rolled over, and sat up. I had no idea what time it was, where I was, or what I should do next. I just sat there. As I was pulling myself up, a couple of sailors were walking by so I called out to them to ask for a little help. I told them my money was gone and I needed to get back to the Midway. I asked if they could spot me. Fortunately for me, they were sharing a cab back to the USS Blue Ridge, our battle group flag ship.

For the rest of the Korea tour I decided to focus my time on work, conducting collection and evaluation assessments of intelligence regarding the indigenous people and the Olympic Games instead of liberty or the indulgence of a port call. We were scheduled to pull out soon and head back to Yokosuka, Japan for a short six-month dry-dock period. I decided to make an appointment with the ship's chaplain. I needed to talk out my thoughts, heartaches, and concerns about my relationship with God versus being a typical sailor during these port calls. After sitting down with him I was in shock of his position as a minister, a professional counselor, and a protestant believer. I tried to explain to him that I was struggling in my heart and mind with purity. I told him I was married and wanted to feel like I was being an honorable husband. I thought that I would get a great spiritual chat on where I needed to be in my walk with God, what I needed to be focusing on, and maybe be a lesson or two on living righteously. Maybe he'd give me a couple of Bible study groups to attend. But no, it was not the case at all. He took a different approach. He told me how my thoughts and problems are normal and that it would probably help if I relaxed and just accepted it as a problem that couldn't be fixed.

Additionally, he told me that I should consider picking up Playboy magazines and instead of looking at the pictures, try to concentrate on the great articles. He also gave me his textbook knowledge of how the Navy's divorce rate is reaching 75% among shipboard sailors. I told him I thought he would try to request an immediate transfer to a shore billet so I could be with my wife and build my marriage. He said no, he wasn't going to request that as there had to be a better reason. I replied, "Sir, you are signing off divorce papers and conducting one-sided marital counseling. You just told me that 75% of the shipboard sailors are experiencing divorce. Don't you think the Navy should try a new program?" I then asked, since he couldn't approve my request for early shore duty would he approve a request that I bring my wife to Japan while we are in our six-month dry-dock period. Again, he said no. I was an E4 and could only do that if I was an E5 or above. Also, this deployment was considered a remote tour. I went away from my time with this chaplain in utter disbelief and disappointment. I was confused as this wasn't the Christianity that I read about from Keith Green's book, nor was it the type of Christianity that I was learning in the Bible.

Angry, confused and unsure about what I needed to do, I decided to write my wife, Amy. I asked her if she would be willing to come over for a few months while we were in our dry-dock period. I had to let her know that I was going against the Navy regulation due to my rank and deployment status. I didn't have a place for us to live and I wasn't sure if I could even afford it, but if she was willing to come over I would find a place somehow. She wrote back and agreed, so I began to look for a place. After about two weeks I secured a house that I would be sharing with another sailor that I met when I had previously worked with the engineering department. Steve had married a girl from the UK that he met in a bar in one of the ports we had visited. He was an E5 and lived in a house about three miles outside the base in the local economy. Amy and I would rent a room he had for a share of the rent.

Amy flew to Japan and we got settled into our new place with this other couple. I had not seen her for a few months. We had a great few days getting acquainted with each other and getting her oriented to the base and the Japanese culture. Little did I know that our department would go to Port and Starboard duty. Port and Starboard duty consisted of one day on, working a 24-hour shift and one day off. Being in dry dock caused the intel shop to have less work so we were often farmed out to ops or another department to work on the ship. I ended up, along with others, working with the deck department chipping or painting the side of the ship and bringing the ship to the required scheduled restoration. I was so discouraged. Here I had paid for my wife to come over to a foreign country and live in a different culture. I wanted both of us to build our marriage and create something that we didn't have. We lived with another couple so there was no privacy. We spent every bit of my paycheck on the rent and utility bills we had to pay to Steve and his wife, which they used to buy new furniture and build their home with nice things. Amy ended up applying for a job at the McDonalds on base to help with our money situation. The worst of all was I barely got to see her. Every other day I would get off. I would have about 8 hours with her, then I slept before I went to my duty for the next 24 hours, leaving her alone.

After about three months we had completed our dry dock period ahead of schedule and the captain desired to conduct sea trials. We were scheduled for two weeks out and two weeks in to make repairs and then back out for more sea trials for two weeks. The main purpose of the dry-dock period was to add blisters to the ship's side which provided more stabilization to the ship while under way. So, while the ship was being built up and worked on, my marriage was suffering. During one of the sea trial periods Amy moved out of the house to stay with a lady she barely knew because her relationship with Steve's wife was getting unbearable. Once

Where I Belong

back at sea, Amy went back to the States to stay with her family until my tour ended in Japan.

Later I flew out to meet back up with her. I was in the Philippine Sea. I flew off the carrier to Subic Bay where I caught a cab and traveled two hours up to Clark Air Base near Manila. It was not a great trip. I was tired from flying off the carrier at an odd a.m. hour and then waiting for the cab to pick me up. Jumping on helicopters to run Snoopy Operations wasn't a problem but flying off a short carrier flight deck while bouncing up and down on the ocean was a different trick. From there it got worse. My cab happened to be yellow.

This would have been a key piece of traveling information if I would have been following the last couple of years of Philippine elections. In 1986, the Philippine president, Marcos, was going through a coup d'état due to his poor leadership and pilfering of state funds. His government was eventually overthrown. His opponent, Corazon Aquino, the wife of the late Benigno Aquino (who ran against Marcos in earlier elections and was mysteriously assassinated). Therefore, Aquino supporters and party members had Corazon run and then placed her in power. Two years into her campaign, she held district elections for governors which erupted into major party divisions. Aquino's campaign color was yellow, which made her stand out.

My yellow cab traveled through an area that, unbeknownst to me, was pro Marcos. We experienced a light ambush with pro-Marcos supporters throwing rocks at our van. The windshield was cracked and when we slowed down we would get bats beaten against the doors. Till this day, I have no idea how we made it to Clark AB in one piece, but we did. While at Clark, I had to wait on standby for 12 hours to catch a flight to Guam, then to Hawaii then to Travis AB in California. From there I took a cab to LAX and booked a flight to Milwaukee to meet up with my wife. We visited her grandparents then we traveled 14 hours down to NC. It was the longest four days of my entire life.

We spent the Christmas holidays, the first one I had off in three years, with her family in the mountains of NC. Then Amy and I packed up our small Honda and traveled across country to Texas for a four-month stopover for an advanced intel school. While there, we lived in a two-room

71

apartment and found a nice little Texas church to attend. Our lives seemed to take some shape, and we began to actually feel married. After completing my intel training we packed up again and drove the rest of the way across the States to California where we would ship our car off to our new duty station, Hawaii. I was to report to Intelligence Pacific Command (IPAC) located at Camp Smith on the island of Oahu. My new job had titled me South East Asia Analyst and Staff Briefer. I would end up briefing CINCPACFLT (Commander Pacific Fleet) every other morning at 0600. I would later be moved to Hickam AB to conduct Tomahawk cruise missile targeting of targets in the emerging second Gulf War.

Amy and I struggled to find a church that would meet our needs. We just wanted to grow as Christians, be productive people and move forward with our lives. We visited several churches while also listening to a Christian radio station called KLHT found at 1040 on the AM dial. Its broadcast format was primarily Bible teaching. I remember listening to this old timer called J. Vernon Magee. He had a country twang, yet his words were life to me as he taught simply through the Bible. I would listen for hours when I could. I fell in love with one other teacher that really spoke inwardly to my heart. I was so enamored with his style of teaching which was simply verse by verse. His name was Mike MacIntosh. Mike was the pastor of Horizon Christian Fellowship out of San Diego, CA. He had been mentored and schooled by Chuck Smith, a well-known pastor out of Southern California pastoring at a church called Calvary Chapel Costa Mesa.

Pastor Chuck was well known for his verse by verse style of teaching and his complete reliance of the Holy Spirit to move through God's Word. He was equally famous for being the most instrumental person during the Jesus movement, being willing to listen and minister to the hippies in and around Southern California.

Chapter 7

AWARDED

In late 1989, IPAC had assigned me to the Southeast Asia desk where I would monitor and analyze strategic movement in those third world countries. Being the new kid on the block, I got the territory that nobody wanted. I begged and positioned myself for a more active and hostile area within one of the Soviet Communist Blocs. Within a few short weeks I had earned my place as one of the lead analysts reporting on Ballistic Missile sub movements out of major Russian ports. Portions of my time were divided among monitoring, reporting, and preparing to brief the Four Star CINCPACFLT Admiral each morning on new intel items of interest.

At the time, Poland and Hungary were experiencing civil unrest due to political riots stemming from a peaceful student demonstration. This would in turn cause daisy chain effects throughout the other Communist Bloc countries. As social unrest began to unfold, East Germany's political party was also unraveling. Just three years prior, in 1987, US president, Ronald Reagan, stood in front of the Brandenburg Gate, an entrance from Western Berlin into Eastern Berlin, Germany's Communist territory, and declared openly and boldly to the USSR's president, Mikhail Gorbachev:

"General Secretary Gorbachev, if you seek peace, if you seek prosperity for the Soviet Union and Eastern Europe, if you seek liberalization: Come here to this gate! Mr. Gorbachev, open this gate! Mr. Gorbachev, tear down this wall!"

The culmination of Ronald Reagan's haunting speech reverberating throughout Communist Europe and the mounting displeasure of the oppressed people resulted in imminent change. In 1989, Eastern Berlin opened its gates for free access to the those living in Western Berlin.

No one expected what followed. Thousands gathered on and around the Berlin Wall with hammers and began pounding away, eventually knocking it down.

One of my best friends, Les was stationed in Berlin with a classified special operations detachment during the Cold War. He was in the thick of the chaos while portions of the wall were coming down. Much of their work was "snatch and grab" operations of high profile individuals and known war criminals among other persons of interest (POI). This clandestine detachment was known as the action arm of the CIA's Special Activities Division (SAD). Ironically, Les and I would connect years later under different circumstances while working as a cut-out for SAD. However, at the moment, the Cold War era was ending.

Intelligence gathering was changing as we watched communist Europe get free from Marxism. Due to satellite technology and the advent of computers, to include the internet, the Cold War methods of Human Intelligence (HUMINT) as a priority was shifting to Imagery Intelligence (IMINT). HUMINT was not disappearing, it was just not going to be a priority. The US Government was spending billions of dollars on satellite imagery platforms. We could now see what our foes were doing without having to spin up a pool of human assets to get information for us. I had moved from Maritime and Operation Intelligence (OPINTEL) to IMINT, which kept me at the cutting edge of the collection, gathering, and dissemination game, at least at the strategic level. I soon moved to another command as part of a shift of Intelligence Priorities (IP). My location would be classified in a large hanger on Hickam AFB in Hawaii. I shifted from monitoring and reporting to targeting key installations in the Middle East. Hundreds of targets in Iraq would filter through my desk where I would be required to locate, identify, and pinpoint key targets belonging to Saddam Hussein and his Baath Party regime.

On one mid-week afternoon, as I was studying imagery of some vehicles pulling SCUD missiles outlined on an Iraqi road in formation heading northwest toward the Syrian border, I was interrupted by several gentlemen standing next to my light table. With some frustration, I lifted my eyes off the scopes and glanced at the men next to me. It was Captain Jacoby with several of his aides and my boss, an Air Force major. Captain

Jacoby was in fact everyone's boss in the intelligence community in the Pacific Rim. He was the Director of Intelligence for the Joint Intelligence Command Pacific (JICPAC). He would later become a member of the Joint Chiefs of Staff, and once promoted to Admiral, he would become the Director of the Defense Intelligence Agency (DIA), which I would work for under his direction in years to come.

As I stood there exchanging formal greetings and exercising normal military protocols, the captain asked what I was working on. I took the opportunity to jokingly say, "Sir, my work is highly classified, on a need-to-know basis only. If I tell you, I would have to kill you." My boss, the major, was glaring me down, in disbelief that I would even joke around with an officer of Jacoby's stature, but the captain laughed, and then all the aides and the major laughed. I gave him a brief synopsis of what I was tracking with the SCUD missiles and how the Iraqi's were purportedly moving their arms westward. He was genuine in his comments and inquiry. After a couple of other questions and answers, his aide stated that there was a citation that needed to be awarded. The major then stated, "Attention to orders!" I popped to attention and looked forward. The aide read the citation aloud and Captain Jacoby handed me the framed award and reached to shake my hand. Without me knowing it, the citation was for some intelligence work that I had done weeks before on collecting information on a reported weapons factory in Iraq. This information had been miss-reported and miss-identified by someone else, and I figured their findings to be gross errors. The identity of the factory was in fact a milk processing plant that was next to a school, and I reported it as such, despite the previous report.

As the admiral shook my hand, he looked at me and said, "Petty Officer Cunningham, it is outstanding work like this that gives me goose bumps to serve in the United States Navy. Your accurate attention to detail not only saved the US Government millions of dollars had we attacked Iraq, but you also saved countless kids' lives, giving them a hope for the future." I thanked the captain and his aides, and they departed my work-space. I just sat there in awe of the moment. I just got an award from the highest intelligence official in the Pacific Rim, plus, I was astounded that I did something that someone would notice. I was just doing my job and barely remembered that target until they brought it up. My supervisor, Steven LeBlanc, a Sargent in the Air Force, and my co-worker, another Air Force member, were equally as shocked as they stood beside their desks. I just looked at them both, chuckled, and said, "What can I say, but Go Navy!" They laughed and made their way over to my desk to check out the award.

It was 1990 and Operation Desert Shield and Desert Storm were just heating up. All my targeting work was a result from the earlier conflict, the Gulf War. I had been involved with several conflicts, directly or indirectly. My work was becoming more mundane and I just needed something a little more operational. I had another year plus before I was going to come up on orders and was deciding whether I was going to stay in. I had forgone the idea to drop my papers for EOD training at the request of my wife. She just wanted me to come home at the end of the day, and she wanted to be sure of it. I was chained to my desk, finding targets, briefing the boss, and still trying to figure out what to do with my life. I was growing increasingly impatient with my spiritual growth, not satisfied with any churches that Amy and I visited. One day as I was driving home, I turned my radio dial to 1040 AM and began listening to KLHT radio. After the program, I heard an announcement that Mike MacIntosh was going to be in Honolulu speaking at the Blaisdell Arena that night.

I was so excited, as soon as I got home and told Amy that Mike MacIntosh was going to be speaking downtown in a couple of hours and I wanted to get ready and go. We ate, fed the dog, and headed downtown to listen to Mike teach out of the Bible. I remember listening and taking notes on what Mike was sharing. It was as if he was making the Bible come alive for me in our current day. Some would say it was prophetic. My soul was enriched, and I hated that the teaching had to stop. We stopped by the product table where I picked up a copy of Mike's book, *For the Love of Mike*, to read later. Amy and I made our way out to the car and began to pull out of the street parking space when my eye caught Mike in front of the Blaisdell's doors speaking with someone. I cut off the car and told Amy that I needed to talk to him. She asked me what I was going to say, and I told her, "I don't know, I just know that I need to talk to him." We got out of the car and made our way up to the door where Mike was still speaking and stood by until he was done. We stepped up and introduced ourselves. I thanked Mike for the message and handed him my book to get him to sign it. I began to explain to him my journey of coming to know Christ and how we were suffering from not being able to find a decent church to get involved and grow in. Mike began to tell us about a couple of churches on the east side of the island and then paused and said, "No wait, down the road here in the middle of town is a Calvary Chapel in an old theater. The pastor is Bill Stonebraker, an old surfboard shaping legend." He wrote it out in the back of the book and told us to check it out. He laid his hands on our shoulders and prayed for us, asking God to direct our paths and give us strength to walk with him each day. He also prayed that if we go to Calvary Chapel downtown, God would speak to our hearts and help us to mature in our faith.

Amy and I left there very encouraged. I had never really had anyone pray for us like that, standing in the middle of a public arena. It was refreshing, and it seemed to strengthen me. That following Sunday we visited Calvary Chapel in downtown Honolulu. I had driven by it several times and thought that it wasn't the place for me. It was in the heart of downtown in front of the red-light district. I just thought that it would not have what I was looking for in a church. Yet, per Mike's recommendation, I was going to give it a shot. We went to the morning Sunday service. As we walked in, the foyer was a little narrow and the sanctuary was an old movie theater with some modifications. My first experience of the service was unimpressive. I seemed to critique everything around me and not focus on the message that Pastor Bill Stonebraker was delivering. We left and decided that we were going to try another church that was down the road that had a large following. The next week, we went to the church and found ourselves in the middle of a very charismatic message about giving and getting blessing out of what you are able to give. I kept thinking throughout the message that there are some here that are able to give more, therefore, their blessing will be more. Yet, if I give according to my small navy salary, then I would only be blessed per what I give. It just didn't seem to jive with me for some reason. The speaker was very persistent and lively about what he was saying. He got to a point in the sermon when he said that there are those here that can't understand His anointed message and that they will walk out without being blessed. At that point, I grabbed my wife's hand, stood up and made my way to the end of the aisle. We walked up to the front, passed by the podium, walked between the congregation and the preacher, and walked out the opposite side door. I was trying to make the point that I did not want to be blessed by that guy's message or even attempt to agree with what he was saying. Either I did not understand, or it was just a bunch of hoopla.

The next week, I prayed, and God told me to go back to Calvary Chapel in Honolulu and prepare my heart to hear from Him and not focus on how things were done around me. We did just that. Amy and I stayed there and began to grow in understanding of what the Bible was all about. It's as if God's voice was speaking to us. The once a week gathering turned into twice a week, then three times a week. We added a Bible study in our home and additionally got involved as a volunteer in one of the ministries called YDI.

YDI stood for Youth Development Inc. It was a ministry Mike McIntosh had developed to meet the needs of the growing run-away youth population. YDI also had a run-away hotline called 1-800-HIT-HOME which was a crisis counseling ministry for any run away that needed help and wanted to get off the streets. Amy and I dedicated ourselves to this ministry over the next year. We went through the counseling course which entailed understanding how and what resources were available when teenagers called. Every Saturday night around 8 pm, Amy and I and a couple of other folks would go to the church and receive any incoming calls from run-away teenagers from all over the nation. YDI ensured that they were pushing out business cards to churches that desired to participate in this program. These churches in turn would flood their cities with these cards that had the 1-800-HIT-HOME number on it for any teenager that wanted help to get off the streets. I thought we would have just a couple of folks call from time to time, but that was not the case. It seemed that we had call after call from kids who were living on the streets, strung out on drugs, destitute, without a home, confused, heartbroken, and making a living by prostituting themselves for food, drugs, or other needs. Whether it was girls or guys, they were finally at a place where they truly wanted. Frankly, it was a life changing experience for me, as I didn't know how bad and broken some of these kids were all over the nation.

Chapter 8

VW's AND PORSCHES

I continued working on classified projects for the Department of Defense, specifically on the region of Iraq, and taking on morning briefing for CINCPACFLT while also serving in the ministry. During this ministry period I sensed a heaviness to do more but I knew I wasn't equipped to fulfill that desire. I wanted to do more for God. I had a fire and I did not want the flame to dwindle down. My wife was asked to come on staff as a receptionist at our church while I signed up for the School of Ministry to learn more about helping serve people. The School of Ministry (SOM) was a yearlong program that was geared toward those that wanted to serve or fill ministry gaps. The idea was to train men and women on how to hear and understand God's voice. It was intended to make one grow in his or her faith. It changed my life. I never knew God until I began to study about him for myself. I knew about him, but didn't know him.

In 1991, my wife was reaching the full term of her first pregnancy. We had been trying to start a family, and now our first child was getting ready to be born. I struggled greatly with the idea of being a father. I just knew that I was going to be horrible. I was haunted. Amy woke me up early one morning and told me it was time to get ready to go to the hospital. I was a little delirious and began to clean up the bedroom and wash clothes until she alerted me how serious she was about getting to the hospital. Once we arrived we were placed in a room for monitoring. She had just recently told me that she figured out what she wanted to name the him, Christian Josiah. A young doctor came in and checked her out and realized her water had broken and she was going to deliver very soon. The doctor had her placed in bed and wheeled her down to the delivery room. I wandered around the halls just waiting and within minutes the doctor and about three nurses were wheeling my wife down the hallway again in panic mode. I asked what was wrong as they were going by me and the nurse just said that there were complications and they have to do an emergency C-Section to save the baby. Fear came all over me. My wife continued down the hall with tears flooding down her face. I heard her scream out, "Jesus, I need a miracle!" That was the last I saw her for the next few minutes.

I was all bound up inside, worried and full of fear so I called my friend Dan Mantel, the worship leader, to pray for me. Before Dan was finished, I was interrupted by a nurse and asked to come in to be with my wife. I hung up on Dan and allowed her to lead me in the operating room. She explained to me that Christian was turned around backwards and there was no time to turn him. She went on to explain that everything was too far along to do a C-Section. In addition, the umbilical cord was wrapped around Christian's neck cutting off his circulation. All we could do was wait for Amy to deliver and hope that we could resuscitate him in a timely manner. Because Christian was folded up like a jack-knife, his birth was more dangerous than we knew. He came out blue as can be. They brought him over to the table and resuscitated him. I went over to the table and cut the rest of the umbilical cord, picked him up, and whispered to him, "Christian Josiah, you are a miracle."

My wife taught me two things that day. The first was the importance of sacrifice. I was, and still am, amazed at her ability to sacrifice so much for others to live and have life all around her. The second and most remarkable lesson I learned from her was the ability to believe in miracles. I never really believed. I was more of one that excused things away. She showed me something so powerful and so real that it catapulted my faith in God to unmeasurable limits. Even to this day, I think about that point of time and it brings tears to my eyes, not only because of that moment, but for every moment before that where God was truly working out natural ordinary circumstances in extraordinary ways.

As we settled into family life with our newborn, I was also finishing up the SOM and contemplating what I would do next. My time in the Navy was coming to an end. I had to do one of the following: go back to another carrier, submit my package to work at an embassy as an intelligence asset, or get out altogether after fulfilling my commitment. The sea duty did not appeal to me at all. I had been there and done that. I was offered an opportunity to go to Madagascar's U.S. Embassy where I would be an intelligence reports writer, but this was a little misleading. The recruiter made it sound like I would be assisting case officers on their "wine & dine" circuit as they conducted collections during embassy dinners. That was a job for Navy intel guys but it usually was for E7's and above. I was an E5 at the time. I heard through someone else that the job I would have as a reports writer was actually sitting on a pier or a boat in the burning hot Madagascar sun. I would count ships coming into port and make note of who they were and what flag they were sailing under. Of course, there would be other noteworthy observations that needed to be addressed such as the ship's level as it pulls into port and the level it pulls out at, any cargo or container count, any identifiable antennas, and other electronics. This information and a slew of pictures would accompany the report.

After some time of consideration, I chose to leave the Navy. It just didn't appeal to me any longer. I felt that I had put my wife through enough pain with my Navy career. I had a family now and needed to spend time with them. I also felt that I had a new mission, a new war to fight, which was living a life for God. It began to hit me during my time in SOM. One of my instructors, Heath Habbeshaw, was teaching on the life of David. He spoke something to me that struck a chord. He stated after sharing about the difference of Saul hiding away from Goliath and David going after Goliath, that "God is looking for men to stand in the gap." I felt that was a message to me.

As I made plans to get out of the Navy I began to pray about going back to Asheville, NC to start a Bible study in my home with the intent of planting a church. I would work a job during the day and begin to minister in my community. It seemed like a great plan. After all, many other Calvary Chapel pastors started out that way. My own pastor, Bill Stonebraker, worked as a surf board shaper and hosted a home Bible study in his house. My distant mentor, Mike McIntosh, got saved off acid and began to minister in half-way houses that Pastor Chuck Smith started called Maranatha House. He then started a fellowship in San Diego. As I figured, there was not much of this style of church or worship going on in the east coast, especially a verse by verse, book by book teaching of the Word of God. I was going to be the next Calvary pastor to plant a great work of God and watch the east coast explode with a revival like no other. With the way I could hear God's voice better than others, why wouldn't a revival break out?

As these great plans were being formed over time, a friend and assistant pastor on staff came to me one day after completing my last SOM class. His name was Derald Skinner. Derald came from Raul Ries church in West Covina, CA. Raul was popular in the Calvary Chapel movement. He tried to kill his wife and himself until God got a hold of him while he was sticking a gun to his head. He had the TV on and Chuck Smith happened to be talking about the grace of God. Raul was so moved by the message that he put down the gun and surrendered his life to Christ at that moment. Raul later wrote a book about his life called "Fury to Freedom." A movie version followed years later._{ii} Derald came to me and asked if I would like to come on staff and oversee the children's ministry and the radio ministry called "As We Gather." They wanted to offer me an assistant pastor position. I knew I needed some mentoring and coaching. I jumped at the opportunity despite some family concern.

We had been in Hawaii for three and a half years and had told Amy's family that we would probably being moving back soon. Her dad's health was slowly declining. He had multiple-sclerosis and went through bouts of sickness. He had a 1964 Mustang Fast-Back, black with red interior. It was a great looking car. He had offered me the car if I brought his little girl back home. To add more pressure, her family owned about 60 acres up in the hills of Western North Carolina just minutes outside of Asheville. He offered me 3 acres of that land as an alternative if I didn't want the car. I turned down Amy's father's offers and decided to stay in Hawaii. With that in mind, I had a few more weeks to finish up in the Navy, check out, and find an apartment. Amy and I found a nice little condo on the east side of the island in a place called Hawaii Kai. The condo was right on a canal running into the ocean. A perfect little place to start raising my family.

Over the next ten years I made it a point to live up to my new position as a pastor. My personality was such that I had to accomplish

82

something, and when I accomplished something it had to be big. My first go-big-or-go-home opportunity happened after I took over the children's ministry. For Vacation Bible School at church that first year, I turned the entire church into a fort with large card board boxes (refrigerator size) spread throughout different places, making tunnels and hide outs. We dressed up as characters in the Bible and played their parts. I played Abraham and disguised my voice as an old patriarch telling the amazing story of how faithful God was to the kids that came. As we did the VBS theme in the church I recall some of the staff and board members coming around. I noticed that some did not know what to make of it; some liked it, but others thought it was a bit much, as we had other services going on throughout the week too.

When I took over the radio ministry, I wanted to take the broadcast from airing on 5 stations to hundreds of stations. We ended up getting it on about 200+ stations across America within the nine years that I served there. Most of the success came from another church purchasing a transponder station from a network that was rapidly growing called CSN or Calvary Satellite Network (now called Christian Satellite Network). The "As We Gather" radio ministry was truly a God send in my life. I learned how to digitally master or mix speaking messages. While doing this, God's Spirit was speaking to me, growing my faith in ways I did not realize at the time. Bill Stonebraker's messages were intellectually appealing, yet there was a simple Godly theme that was threaded through each message.

As 1992 to 1994 rolled around, the church was beginning to grow. More people were asked to come on staff to help minister in the community and at the church. Stan, one of my best friends, came on board to take over the children's ministry. It was a little bit of a shock to me at first but I understood that growth was taking place and each ministry needed an overseer. In my heart of hearts, it bothered me. It wasn't because Stan was taking over what I was doing. He was perfect for the job. He was a super nice and happy guy with an actual teaching background. My concerns were with me. I wanted to do it all, ie Children's ministry, radio, Bible studies, media library and so on. Nonetheless, it was a good move to have him on board. We were not only busy with church growth but also with conferences. Our church hosted Greg Laurie's Harvest Crusades in the

Islands. On top of that, we planned a pastor's conference, a "How to Walk" conference, and an "End Times" conference, all in the same week. Greg would do his crusades at University of Hawaii's Rainbow Stadium on Friday and Saturday nights. During the day, Saturday, we would have an all-day Christian growth conference called "How to Walk." Sunday, we would do our morning message where we usually asked Greg or Chuck Smith to speak. On Sunday night we would kick off our End Times messages and would continue them every night until Thursday. During the day, beginning on Monday and running through Thursday, we would have the pastor's conferences going on. Each year we did this, and it was a huge endeavor, yet very rewarding as we had the opportunity to meet popular Christian music artists and speakers like Switchfoot, DC Talk, OC Supertones, and Big Tent Revival. The speakers were Gayle Ewrin, Chuck Missler, Chuck Smith, Greg Laurie, Skip Hietzig, Jon Couson, Mike McIntosh, Don McClure and Bob Coy.

Although this may seem superficial to mention all this, I would have to say it was a great experience to work with these other people as it was a labor of love. There were two important moments during these events that changed the course of my beliefs about ministry and would gnaw on me for the next 20+ years. The first moment was when I was experiencing a period of being overwhelmed and made mention of it to one of Greg Laurie's assistants, John Collins. John was Greg's "go to" guy. John would come into town before any event and get things going and would stay until everything was completed. He observed that I was having some personal struggles putting my portion of the events together and just listened to my concerns. He prayed for me and went on his way. A couple of days later he came into the church office and gave me a book titled "The Making of a Man of God" by Alan Redpath. The book was about how God allowed David's life to be pressed or crushed in order to use him as God's man to lead the people of Israel. John had written a note inside the cover of the book, "Will, God will only use you when you are broken and humble before him. Blessings, John." It was something that I came to cherish as I read because John took the time to actually minister to me and not just go about ministry business. I would have to say that I learned more from that moment than most of the years I spent in ministry. It made a huge impact on me.

The second moment that impacted me was during a time when Don McClure was sharing a message. He shared on the life of Jacob when he wrestled with God. I hung out with Don after the message and mentioned to him that his message really spoke to me. Don ended up praying for me and my growth in the ministry. I think it spoke so deeply to me as I was grasping to find my identity in ministry and wrestling with God about it.

I began to step out in faith and take on new responsibilities. Between 1995 and 2000 I struggled with the question, "What's next?" Derald decided to move and plant his own church on the other side of town. Another person volunteering in the ministry was James. He took a leap of faith and moved his entire family to Iowa and planted a church there. A young surfer from California came over and attended our church for a short bit and planted a church in Molokai, a small island near Oahu. Charles, another friend I met in the ministry, moved westward and planted a church there. Two other churches were also planted in Maui and Kauai. I was experiencing and witnessing a work of God in men's lives and they were moving forward to do the work of God. It wasn't only church planting locally; missions expanded as well. My friend, David, started a new missionary post in the South Pacific in Vanuatu. Another couple planted a church in Japan along with two other couples. Bud Stonebraker, Bill's son, had spent some time in Hungary and led a group there as part of the mission outreach for the church. We also were making regular trips to Russia on missionary endeavors since the Iron Curtain had dropped.

My stepping out in faith was more of a push to mask my insecurity in ministry. I felt I wasn't doing enough or could do better, which may or may not have been true, but the real problem was a lack of power in my life. I knew how to put together a Bible study and began teaching in my home on a weekly basis. We had moved into a bigger house which was perfect for our Friday night fellowship. We had three to six couples that would come out each week.

Additionally, Tom Mauch, a volunteer on staff, was retiring from coaching tennis at Punahou School, an elite private high school. He had taken on teaching and directing the small satellite Bible college that Calvary Chapel began about a year before. Tom was asked by Chuck Smith of Calvary Chapel Costa Mesa to move to California and help him in

85

establishing the new main campus of the Calvary Chapel Bible College in Hot Springs, California. As a result, Tom asked me to take over the Bible college.

We were a small extension of the main campus in Twin Peaks California with about 25 students at our location. On top of taking over the Bible college I also started a Saturday "Bible Hike" where I would lead folks on hiking trails throughout the island. Once we got to the top of a mountain, I would share a devotion. Additionally, I was being asked to travel and speak for other pastors that were either taking a break or on church business. In these years, I had a lot going on. In reality, I was struggling greatly in my soul. I wanted so bad to be one of the other pastors that was planting a church. I knew I could do it, but my heart was not right. I did not see that until years later. I had the home fellowship, taught and directed the Bible college, led Bible Hikes, spoke at other churches, directed the <u>As We Gather</u> radio program and did my best to maintain a family and do regular duties at church. In all that doing, I had lost the ability of being. That is, being a husband and father. No matter how hard I tried to balance the two lives, I was too busy trying to be something else, and my family suffered because of it.

When time permitted, I would take my wife and kids to the beach or hike Coco Crater in Hawaii Kai, just on the other side of Sunset Beach. We were coming back from a walk one day and I saw a dog trying to attack a duck. I jumped in the water to save the duck from its predator. My kids thought I was a super hero. There was another time I was taking my oldest son on a hike up the crater. He slipped on the rocky trail and began to fall off the side. I ran to him, grabbed his arm, and pulled him up in the nick of time from disaster. He was just 6 or 7 years old at the time. I remember telling him as I looked down the large cliffs to the bottom, "Son, God has a plan for your life." As the words left my mouth, I remembered that my mother had spoken to me some years before in Mars Hill, North Carolina. Her words never left me.

When I was 16, I was driving back from having dinner with a cute girl I was dating at the time. Sasha was taking ballet lessons then. As I was driving her home from ballet in the pitch-black night, it began to snow, and I hit a slick patch in the road. I lost control of the car and went over a steep hill, flipping the car several times, tearing it to pieces. Sasha was thrown to the back and I was thrown under the dash board. We were both banged up but okay. We climbed out of the car and began to hike our way back up the hill with the car wheezing behind us. We flagged down a car and were taken to the sheriff's office and later to the hospital. Two or three days later I asked my Mom to take me to the crash site so I could figure out what I needed to do about the car. When we arrived there, I began looking over the hill I had tumbled down and saw the car torn up and the engine hanging partially out. Windows were busted and the roof caved in. I stood there bragging about how I survived rolling the car. I was kind of cocky about it. I turned around to brag more to my Mom. She stood there with tears flooding down her face. I said "Mom, don't be sad, I am ok," and tried to put my arms around her to hug her. She shrugged me off and held me in front of her face and said, "You listen to me! You need to know that God has a plan for your life." It was one of those heart-throbbing, throat-gulping, goose-bump moments you only see in movies with the music playing in the back ground. Part of me thought Mom was just being concerned, but more of me knew that she recognized something so real to her that she wanted me to hear it. Looking back now, I wonder if God used that moment in her life to reveal how real He was, as the wreck was pretty bad. That same moment came back to me as I spoke those exact words to my young son Christian. "Son, God has a plan for your life! I don't know what it is, but He has a plan for you!" He and I hiked back down and went home. He ran in the house telling his mother how I had saved his life. I got in trouble for not keeping a closer eye on him.

As I thought back on those moments, both when I was a teen and rescuing my son, I realized that God did have a plan for me. I would have never thought I would be in the ministry some 12 to 15 years later. I would have never dreamed of having kids and living in Hawaii. I would have never imagined that I would be married to a beautiful blonde gal who never gave up hope on me. During this period in my life I realized that I was taking a lot of things for granted. Although I didn't pull back anything, I began to pursue and write a personal study on the lives of those that were proud and how God humbled them in order that he could use them. I titled it, "Lifestyles of the Boastful and Broken." It was a look at biblical characters that were filled with pride and how God broke their self-righteous spirit. It was a huge lesson for me, but not huge enough.

As the year 2000 was approaching I was still struggling with feeling like I was not meeting up to my full potential and wanted to plant my own church. I wanted to take what I had learned in the ministry here from Bill Stonebraker and see it thrive in Western North Carolina, hopefully Asheville. I felt strongly about it and thought, "God, you wouldn't have invested all this in me to waste it here. I mean, I was teaching in different pulpits, directing the small Bible college and so on. I thought I was God's man for the job, even after doing that study on boastfulness a year before. So I convinced Amy that it was time for us to go. We had been involved with the ministry for over nine years and it was time for me to make space to allow others to yield the same growth. She and I were going to go to North Carolina and start our own church. I had convinced myself I was being sacrificial, but it was all pride.

Bill Stonebraker still couldn't believe that I was going to run off and do all this without requesting any support. He had called me to his office and asked me, "Willie, why do you want to leave? You are like a son to me." That statement really choked me up. Bill was not real familiar with my up-bringing. For him to say that to me was like a cure to cancer. He didn't realize how broken and abusive my background was. I never really shared it with others at all. It was personal to me. I sat there in his office masking the pain of the moment and told him, "Bill, at times I feel like a Porsche mechanic and all I have are VWs to work on." Bill brushed off the statement and tried to encourage me to give it some time and re-think the move. I never realized how stupid my statement must have sounded to him until years later. After all, I was there serving God's people in his ministry, regardless of how good I was or whether I am called to work on Porsches or VWs. How could I ever think so foolishly of myself and God's people. I was blind to my pride at the time and proceeded with my plans to move back across the Pacific and America and plant my church.

As Amy was getting things situated in NC, I was finishing up teaching on the book of Hebrews in the Bible college. I had a couple months or so to go and remember coming across a passage in chapter 2, which taught about drifting away from God. Hebrews 2:1 was a warning,

"Therefore, we must give the more earnest heed to the things we have heard, lest we drift away." It was a reminder that we not take our salvation for granted. I remember praying in my own heart asking God to help me to always be mindful of this. I asked him to let it not be me nor any of my students.

I finished closing up the house we were renting and bounced around a couple of friends' houses to sleep on their sofas until I left for the mainland. Little did I know that this was going to be my lifestyle over the next year.

Chapter 9

DIGGING DITCHES

With no place to live, we had planned to stay with my in-laws for a short period until we could get stabilized. We made three beds out of cots and had another queen bed for Amy and I in the her parents' basement, surrounded by her mom's quilting material and canned goods and her dad's trophy stuffed elk head. It did not bother me much, as I knew it was just temporary. In my mind, I was there to be used by God. I had already worked out a job with the CSN radio network as a manager and Amy would surely find something quickly as she always had. I kept reminding myself of a quote that went around in the Calvary Chapel circles, "Where God guides, He provides." It is a spiritual truth, yet how I was interpreting it would be a life-long lesson that took me by surprise.

After a couple of weeks of relaxing with family, we packed up the van to do an initial visit to Apex, NC. I had recently spoken at a chapel in Columbia, South Carolina as well as a fellowship in Boone, North Carolina. I felt like everything was falling into place as it should. When we got into Apex, I found a pay phone (yes, there was still one around in 2000) and called the CSN coordinator, Rob, to check in and find out where I needed to meet him. Rob cleared his throat and said, "There has been a change in the station in Apex. The leadership has decided to keep it 'dark' as they have purchased another station that would bring in more revenue in Austin, Texas." At that moment, I was speechless. I turned around in the phone booth to look at my wife and kids rustling around in the van and I thought to myself, "What in the hell have I done?" Out of desperation, I told Rob that I would be willing to go to Austin if they needed a manager there. I was willing to forego what I felt called to do, share and teach God's word

91

in North Carolina, to meet my own needs; the heck with God's desire. Rob quietly stated that they already had someone in mind for the Austin position. I then asked, "Rob, what about any other position?" He stated that there was nothing right now. I finally said to him, "Rob, I have sold everything I own, left a great ministry, moved across the Pacific Ocean, traveled across the United States and driven several hours to be here and serve God in this capacity. Now what do I do?" He said, "Will, there are no guarantees here. There never were. Things often shift for the greater needs of the ministry. I am sorry. I would recommend that you check with one of the local Calvary Chapels and see if they could use your help until you figure out what is next."

After hanging up, I turned around again to look at my wife and kids in the van and my heart sank, not only my heart, but my liver, kidneys, rib cage, and every other piece of anatomy that was operating under the law of gravity, as well. I had no words to say, no answer, no verse, no idea to share. I was just done. While my body felt like Jell-o walking back to the van, I felt like I was either on death row heading down the aisle to the electric chair or I was walking through a graveyard in a thick fog, carrying my own casket. I stepped into my van and sat in the seat. I looked at Amy and told her that CSN has made a few changes and the station I was going to be overseeing had decided to remain "dark" until further notice. I told her not to worry, we were going to get through all this, yet, in my heart I was screaming and kicking in rage. I told her we were going to head to Cary, North Carolina, about 15 minutes away and get a hotel for the night and visit a new Calvary Chapel that was being planted there. They were having their first Easter service in a local hotel conference center the next day.

The next morning, we got up, got ready and made our way to visit the new church plant at the hotel. It was a time of lively music followed by an aggressively inspirational message. Afterwards, I asked if I could speak to the pastor. I wanted to share with him what was going on with my calling to plant a church and the CSN debacle. He and I sat down and chatted for 20 minutes. I asked him if he had any room for me here. He stated that he did not at the time. He already had people in place to help him plant other fellowships in and around the city, but if I wanted, I could come and be a part of the church. He then reached into his pocket and gave me a 100 bucks and told me to stay in touch.

I walked away feeling like I had just turned a trick on the streets of Cary. I didn't ask for money, I just wanted to be a part of what God was doing there as a fellow pastor. My hope was that he would have appreciated the fact that I was desiring to help build the kingdom of God and let me know what other needs were in the city, thus helping me get involved somehow. Amy, the kids, and I made our way back to the van and began our trip back to Asheville. Every mile that I traveled back home I got more angry, bitter, and troubled. It was the beginning of me drifting from God, and I didn't even know it. It wasn't a slow process; I was drifting at a high rate of speed like I was at the crest of the descent of Niagara Falls. I was going down and it was going to be hard. My bitterness turned into anger and my anger turned into hate. After hours of driving and coming back home like a dog with his tail between his legs, I had pushed my friends, my church, and my family out. I did not feel like dealing with God on the issue at all. I just could not understand why all this was taking place. Why wasn't God guiding or providing? I did not only drift in circles, I made the plunge to go over the falls.

Back in Asheville, I pushed forward and visited another couple of local Calvary Chapels and was told the same thing. "Sorry, there is a work of God already being done here, you are welcome to sit in our services." In my head, I understood this, but in my heart, I didn't. The comments and the gestures pushed me further away, and I drifted more and more. We did decide to settle down at a small, growing chapel of about 100 people located about 17 miles or so from Asheville in the small town of Hendersonville. After several months of attending there, the senior pastor took off for a couple of weeks and the assistant pastor filled in. The assistant pastor decided by the second week of being in charge that it was time for him to take over the ministry. It became a battle for sheep, as some would put it. Amy, myself, and the kids were caught in the middle and felt terrible for the people that were going through the problems with the leadership. We stopped going there and began to search for a new place to fellowship.

After visiting numerous churches and being dissatisfied, I finally went over the falls and drifted into the mist of tumbling water. I had had enough. Asheville is stuck in the middle of the Southeast Bible Belt. The church holds tight to a great deal of tradition, and equally one of the greatest devils of all - the commercialization of Christianity. On one end of the spectrum, you have fundamentalism with the Southern Baptist churches and on the other end you have the charismatic Pentecostals. You dressed up for church. You never wore blue jeans or tee shirts. It was always about what you can do for God and very little about what God has done for you. Every Sunday required an altar call where the pastor would ask for individuals to make Jesus their personal savior. Plain and simple, the theology was twisted in such a way as to appease man's emotions and not glorify God. I knew the Bible taught differently. I couldn't get my foot into the door to minister anywhere, there was no church that my family and I were comfortable with, and frankly I was just mad, disillusioned, and done. I stopped going to church and led my family to do the same.

To make things worse, I had a hard time finding suitable work. I ended up taking a job digging ditches (literally) to lay irrigation in the popular luxury Biltmore development. After a couple of weeks of work and not getting paid on time, I decided it was time to find something else. I landed an hourly job some 50 minutes away working for a man who owned a farm. I got that job through a friend of ours back in Honolulu. It was her brother who happened to have a fabrication plant about an hour from my in-law's home. Still bitter and confused, I argued with God on why all this was happening to me these last few months. I felt as if I was sinking further and further down under the water. Amy was doing okay, she had landed a job with no problems as a legal assistant to a real estate attorney. I was stuck on a farm digging more ditches, running from snakes, feeding cows, and pulling weeds. I had to drive an hour there and an hour back. I was always drained and snappy with the kids. I stopped reading my Bible, stopped going to church and for all intents and purposes, I became a nominal believer. I had lost the fire. It was all about me and survival at this point. God could find someone else. That is how I felt on the outside, but on the inside I was still crying out to Him asking why. I did not know it at the time, but God was still using and shaping me. While working on that farm the owner would send other people over to have me put them to work to help them pay their bills and such. The same thing he was doing for me, he was doing for others.

What was taking place in God's view was opportunities for me to minister to people. I still wanted to serve God and minister His love to people that needed it. Among those that showed up was a young lady who was put out of the Catholic church because she wanted to take communion. They would not let her because she had confessed to getting pregnant without being married. She and I talked for hours while pulling weeds in a flower garden. We chatted about the love of God, what the Bible says about communion, and how God would never put you out of a relationship with Him. Another man was sent over with a back-hoe who was just angry. He had caught his wife in an affair with another man in their church and decided to separate. The man was telling me how he desired to kill his wife and the other guy. He told me that he sees them every Sunday sitting together in the church they all go to, and it made him angry. He came out one morning and was acting out of control with his equipment. It concerned me so much that I stopped him, climbed up on his back-hoe, and said, "Jon, cut this thing off! I know you have had some marriage problems, and it is killing you inside. I used to be a pastor. Would you mind if I prayed for you and your situation?" He looked at me and busted out in tears. I stood there in the middle of this farm on top of this big piece of yellow equipment and put my hand on his shoulder and prayed for God's strength and wisdom to fill him.

There was another time the owner's son came drunk with a bunch of his friends. They had decided to have a party in the house while no one was home. I was too busy on the grounds to notice anything. A few hours later, I was walking up from the barn toward the house and noticed the owner driving up in his Corvette. He ran into the house and started yelling. I went inside and saw the son with a bat and the dad with a gun. They were going to go at it right then and there. For the life of me I can't recall how the situation was defused, but I was able to get the bat and gun in my hands and get the kid out of there. I sat down and chatted with the owner for a bit. I attempted to explain how these things can happen when life is void of God controlling us and we do it ourselves. Later I called the son and invited him to hang out with me for dinner sometime. I let him know that he may just need to talk to someone.

I spent a great deal of time out there on that farm and would often take my kids out there to hang out with me while I would work. I recall taking my oldest son over to a pond on the property to fish. We would cast our lines out into the pond and enjoy both the quiet and surroundings together, until I decided to throw a mega cast into the pond. I threw my rod back as far as I could to cast it hard into the water and as I was getting ready to thrust my arm forward, I looked back and saw that I had accidently hooked my son in the side of his cheek. Next, came wailing and screaming. I had to cut that darn thing out. He often brings it up as a bittersweet experience.

It was not too long after that, while working on that same farm extending a fence line, that I received a call from a lady back in Asheville. She stated her name and asked, "Is this Will Cunningham that went to Madison High School?" I said, "Yes, it is." She began to remind me of a relationship I was involved in with a girlfriend of hers in my high school days. She then told me why she was calling. I had applied for an operation manager's job at a hospitality group and wanted to extend an invitation for an interview. The position was for operational support, as they were opening a new casual dining restaurant in Asheville. I accepted the interview and got the job. God continued to mold me while I continued to buck against good fortune.

I jumped into my new position with eagerness. I hired employees and shift managers, bought supplies, and oversaw construction completion of the store. We kicked off a grand opening and business grew. As time went on, teenagers that I hired began cornering me for advice. They needed a listening ear about parents not understanding, about relationships that were struggling and about future plans. It's as if I was put into a position to provide good counsel to those struggling with life issues. The fact was I was struggling with these life issues also. My parents did not understand me. They were divorced and living separate lives. My mom was finishing up her third marriage; who knew where my father and step-father were? My marriage was good and bad as I never felt worthy to be married or father such great kids. As far as my future...I didn't have a clue at that moment. I was just surviving. I was still mad at God, at my church, and at my family. Yet, I was being used by God in a small way because these kids were seeking some stable answers for their lives.

As I continued working there, I seemed to have no problems keeping the profit and loss statements balanced out. I had a knack for running a business with little to no hiccups. Retention was very good; employees liked working there and they stayed. I followed a philosophy of paying a premium wage for premium service. In other words, you will get an above average wage, but you must maintain an above average performance. Furthermore, inventory was always where it needed to be; I believe in being proactive and preventive. I understood the value of good customer service and how it relates to the value of a dollar. It is important. The owners came in one day, sat me down, and pushed a bonus check to me for a job well done. They told me that I was like Ronald Reagan - always able to cheer the employees on and keep things running smoothly. To this day, I enjoy the comment because I was fond of Reagan.

Although success for me was going well, I still struggled a great deal with not having a father. So, I decided one day that I was going to find my real biological father that hadn't been seen or heard from in 25 years. One of the kids working for me had a mom that was a deputy sheriff, so I asked him if he would ask her to try to locate him for me. I got his birthdate from my mom and his last known address and asked her to do her magic. A few days later she sent a message for me to call her. She had located him in Augusta, South Carolina. He had retired and was living on his own, separated from his second wife.

Augusta was about 45 minutes from Columbia, South Carolina where my mother lived and about 20 minutes from Lexington, SC where my oldest sister lived. For the last 25+ years, no one in my family knew anything of his whereabouts, mainly because no one really cared. However, I was always haunted by the unknown of where he was, what he was doing, whether he was happy or not, and whether he thought of me or my other siblings. After all, I was his kid and wondered if he still loved me. Maybe more accurately stated, wanted him to still love me.

I called my mother up and told her what I had discovered. After receiving a long pause, she asked me, "Chuck, are you sure you want to go down this road?" I told her, "Mom, I have to know. I want him to know that regardless of any and all wrong-doings against us, that they can all be forgiven." There was another long pause. She cleared her throat and told me to give her the number. She would contact him for me to see if it would be ok with him for me to meet him. She was trying to protect me from my other siblings as they would have written me off as their brother.

My mom worked out the details to visit him. I gathered my kids and wife and we went for a long-awaited visit. He lived in a small trailer on about 3 acres in the middle of nowhere in Augusta, South Carolina. He had been in retirement for several years after working for the Pepsi Cola bottling company for over 20 years. He was separated from his second wife and very much alone. We visited him for about two hours, introducing him to my kids and wife and made small talk. I took an opportunity to share with him my testimony of how I came to have peace with God through getting to know Jesus Christ. I also gave him a tape of one of my sermons from years before while serving at Calvary Chapel Honolulu.

After a couple of hours, my family and I got on the road headed back to North Carolina. As I drove home, I experienced a depressing feeling of detachment from my dad. I wanted things to be more than what they were and even more than what I was settling for and yet, I knew that it would never be what the ideal could be. Too many years had gone by. He had his life, and I had mine. There was not much room for disruptions and we both knew it. We would later swap emails on a couple of occasions. I even took another trip down to see him, but he was gone. The trailer was locked up, and he was nowhere to be found. I later came to find out that he was brought up on charges as a sex offender for assaulting an underage girl. Talk about trying to connect to your roots. Needless to say, I was absolutely crushed. At this point I wanted to run and forget it all and figure out how to start completely over. The very man I wanted to reconnect and have a relationship with seemed to continue on in his path of lousy living. I still believe though, in my heart, that he is worth redeeming.

Chapter 10

BACK IN INTEL

It was the latter part of 2001. Months had now passed from seeing my dad and I was pouring myself into work being the best I could be. I made it a point to try to be a great dad. I spent as much time hanging out with my kids as possible. I changed my hours to work in the evenings so I could homeschool the kids in the day time. It was a trick to do it all at one time, but my wife amazingly figured out what they all needed, and I moved forward. While working late one afternoon, I had several customers come in talking about an attack that took place in New York City. I cut on the TV and heard the tragic news of the Twin Towers being attacked, bringing down both buildings, crippling a city, catapulting a nation into great concern, and paralyzing the business market for days. Like many other Americans I felt helpless. The horrific moment will ever live to be known as 9/11. After several months of studying how the media was portraying the US intelligence gathering efforts for the hunt of those responsible for the 9/11 attacks, I decided to not stand by and do nothing. I was also prompted by a question from my eldest son who had asked me one day, "Dad you were one of those intelligence guys, right? Why don't you go help them?" So, I did. After 10 years out of the service, I went back into the Navy as a reservist. The United States Navy wanted qualified and experienced intel professionals. They welcomed me back in, allowing me to keep my former rank and even pushing me a bonus due to the critical manning needs for intelligence gatherers. I would spend the next 9 months (one weekend a month) going through a grueling refresher intelligence course, all the while asking myself, "What did I get myself into?" After the refresher course, I was sent to a two-week intense leadership course at the famed post-graduate Naval School in Monterey, California.

For the life of me, I cannot remember what that leadership course was about nor how I got through it. Frankly it was all beyond me. I do remember successfully completing the course. My buddies and I celebrated by taking a trip to the Pebble Beach Country club to play golf and eat at the clubhouse. It has to be one of the most beautiful drives on Highway 1 (the Pacific Coast Hwy) to the course, which in itself was also a beautiful piece of real estate. Afterwards, we headed back into the town of Monterey to have a couple of celebratory drinks and get a glimpse of the city. My plans were interrupted by a dispute that a man and woman were having on the streets. I told my buddy to hold on, this is something that we can't just walk past. It was a big guy getting into some girl's face about something. She was trying to get away and he would not let her. My mind raced with images of my dad mistreating my mom, and I was compelled to intervene and confront the guy. We began to argue. I was telling him to lay off the girl, and he was telling me to butt out! I maneuvered myself between the guy and girl, putting her behind me and asking my buddy to come escort her to her car. I told the guy that he had two choices, to deal with it as it was being played out and let the girl go, or we would call the cops and let them deal with it. He barked out several threatening comments as he walked away. My buddy, Shane, got the girl to her car, and I walked over and encouraged her to call a girlfriend to come stay with her for the night for her safety. I also told her that she might want to rethink the relationship with that guy. She tried to convince me that he was a great guy, but I wasn't buying it.

After all the training was over I was able to get back to work and make my drill times each month. Another year went by. The owners of my store approached me and asked me if I would be willing to come into a partnership with them. They wanted me to open more stores. I wanted to but really could not afford it. Plus, the liability risk was too great for me at the time. After about a month of contemplating, I told owners that I had to decline the offer. The next day when I went to work I found myself unable to get into the store. The locks were changed so I called the owners to find out what was going on. They told me that they were letting me go; they no longer felt I was a good fit for them. Just like that. One day I was being set up to become a millionaire and the next day, I am shut out, cut off, disregarded. It was a very confusing time. I just could not figure out why I was being treated this way. I could only assume that it was because of business, possibly, to move someone else in as an operating partner as fast as they could.

For the next several weeks, I scrambled to find work. It was around November and I landed a position with a real estate ad company as a sales and operations person. I felt enormous pressure to succeed and not fail. My kids were doing fine, but I was coming undone inside, afraid that I was not able to meet all their needs. My wife and I decided to put our condo on the market. Our first realtor had our condo for 6 months and I decided to drop them due to a lack of activity. It was recommended I go with another family owned broker, Sherrie Puffer, with the Keller Williams Realty Group. She had sold property for my in-laws and came highly recommended. I asked her to come to our place and wanted to interview her on how to sell our property. I told her that I had used another realtor and was very displeased. I would agree to give her our listing on two conditions: one, she would have to let me list it in the real estate publication that I worked for, and two, she would only get my listing for a three-month term, not the six-month term as was usually the protocol. To my surprise Sherrie took the listing under my terms and had the place sold in under 60 days. She was an animal when it came to taking care of her client's needs. She was tenacious and a true professional. She would call me every other week giving me an update and eventually sold our place for the price we were asking.

Sherrie expected her entire Puffer Team to be the same way. She would later stretch out to other housing markets in the Carolinas and turn her residential sales over to her son Brad. He and I became good friends. Although in my late 30's I would have to say that watching her run her business inspired and impressed me. It stirred up a drive in me to excel even more to do the right thing in a timely manner.

We moved back in with my in-laws and began to figure out what to do next. Within a couple of months Amy and I determined that it would be best to move into a rental on the other side of town. It was the week of Christmas of 2003, and we were pulling our items out of storage moving into our new rental. One night, as Amy and I were getting situated, it dawned on me that I could not afford to rent this place and pay for the utilities. So, with much regret and frustration, I approached my wife and told her we couldn't afford this place and we needed to pack up and stay with her parents for a little longer. It was such a grueling night. She and I were at odds with one another. She was confused, and I was angry at myself and the world for my situation. What made things worse is that I had to go back to my in-laws and ask them if we could stay a little longer in their home in the basement. They were very gracious, but I felt like a total failure. I just didn't understand where I was in my life at the time. On one hand, I was succeeding at running a business and doing well with my family. I had even gone back to school to finish off my degree just a year before. On the other hand, here I was a year later, virtually stranded, destitute, and unable to offer my family what they needed in a father and husband. At least that is what I had determined in my own mind.

Meanwhile, President George Bush had been working with the Afghan government. The U.S. government established Operation Enduring Freedom, moving into the country of Afghanistan in an effort to combat the insurgency movement after the 9/11 attacks. He had to help set up the Afghan transitional government by placing Hamid Karzi as a transitional president to stabilize the country as a viable statehood. It was practically listed as a failed state due to the previous Russian occupation and the Taliban tyranny.

It was during the Russian occupation that Usama bin Laden had gotten involved in fighting for the Afghan's freedom. He had joined the Mujahideen movement to fight for Islam and then moved over to Sudan where he would start his al-Qaeda movement. The Taliban formed in the early 90's after Mulla Omar had set a standard in Islamic rule in his own tribe in Kandahar. He started receiving funds from bin Laden to build up the Taliban as a new government. It was a win, win situation for both. The alliance would strengthen the Taliban, formalizing them as a suitable Islamic government and give bin Laden full reign to roam and go as he pleased. President Bush had already requested the Taliban hand over bin Laden as he was currently maintaining safe haven in the region. However, the Taliban did not succumb to Bush's demands and the US, along with

Prime Minister Tony Blair and his British forces, would conduct a series of strikes.

The battle of Tora Bora took place in 2001. Special Forces units chased bin Laden who was on the run. Operation Anaconda was in 2002, where CIA paramilitary personnel and conventional forces would fight Taliban and al-Qaeda members in the mountainous region of the Shahi-kot valley. In 2003, 7th SFG conducted Operation Eagle Fury. The Marines were involved in Operation Asbury Park in 2004. There were 8 operations conducted in 2005 and in 2006, and at least 4 major battles to took place.

This may seem somewhat out of order, yet the point is that I was living in two worlds. Here in the States, I was trying to make a living, and over in Afghanistan I was trying to figure out how I could make an impact. As 2004 rolled around, I became more and more disillusioned with work at the real estate ad company. I ran the local outlet and managed 5 other franchises in the Western Carolina region. My boss told me one night that he didn't know what he would have done if I had not come along. He was thinking about closing the doors and killing himself because his business was going downhill. On the other end of my work some employees were accusing me of having an affair on my wife. It was a ludicrous assumption that someone made because I would have to take off early once a month to go to Atlanta for the Navy drill where my intel unit was. For some reason, a couple of people thought I had a girlfriend down there and that was why I left every month. Frankly, that could not have been any farther from the truth. My wife heard of this by her boss who heard it from someone in my office. Amy came home and laughed it off. She told me that her boss, who was an attorney, was ready to help her file divorce papers on me. I mean, really! Here I was trying to get off each month a couple of hours early to drive 4 hours down to Atlanta in traffic to check into a hotel with another roommate doing the same thing to fulfill drill hours to help make a living and serve my country.

I wanted more than that. More than just living to get by and to fulfill a purpose for someone else. I began to look at some job postings with the Navy and found a position with DIA, the Defense Intelligence Agency. I applied and within a couple of weeks I was interviewed over the phone and subsequently hired. I requested a leave of absence from work to go and take this job with DIA for several months. I didn't know the entire scope of the duties, but I did know that the position was working for a government program in DC called Iraqi Survey Group. The ISG was a joint initiative of the CIA and the DIA. The ISG was essentially a fact-finding mission. Our government was not happy with the UN's progress of searching for weapons of mass destruction, so the U.S. formed an allied version with intelligence professionals from the CIA and the DIA. The ISG had been in existence for over a year and the first two initial reports came back with unfavorable language by the director of the program.

This gig was an exciting chapter in my life. I had seen with my own eyes that there were weapons. I knew where they were and where they were going. I had reported on this in 1990 or '91 while working for the Navy at Hickam Air Force Base. The Navy had a small detachment to work with other military personnel at the Joint Intelligence Command Pacific (JICPAC). There, I was assigned to locate and pinpoint key targets under the Saddam Hussein regime. My office happened to be on the Air Base and not at the main JICPAC HQ.

In my naivety, I thought this would be a no brainer. I would just get looped in on what's been going on and then search for some of those reports from over 10 years ago. I would let the entire intelligence community know what I had found and what border direction the weapons were heading. Surely they would feel the same way I did. I was truly contributing to the dismantling of the axis of evil. This would be far from the truth. I had no idea how enormous the program was.

As I got to DIA and acquainted myself with all the programs attached to the ISG, I began to realize that this was going to be more of a "closed" job than I thought. I couldn't tell anyone who I was working for nor what I was doing. I could say what country I was going to, but not the exact location. At the DIA, I would settle into my location in the basement in the large government building. My direct boss was Col. Jefferies, who was getting me up to speed on what we were doing and how I would fit into the big puzzle. Our boss, and director of the entire program at the time, was the past director of the CIA - George Tenant. Prior to Director Tenant was Director Keith Dayton, who came from the offices of Human Intelligence of the DIA.

Col. Jefferies began to go over a check list of preparation - a tasking that I had to complete before working. The list consisted of going to several different departments to get familiar with the various programs, get a polygraph done, see so and so for identity adjustments and passports, file for my government card to not exceed $25,000.00, get gear at local shop at so and so place, and attend and pass Tactical Operations Training at so and so place. It all started coming together with me in my mind of what was going on. One department I had on my check list was weapons card authorization. I was cleared to carry a concealed weapon anywhere in the US and its responsible dominions. As I was signing off on papers it clicked for me. If I drew my side arm, it was only to render a kill, not to injure, but to kill. At this point, it was clear to me that this was not just some intel analyst job at a high-speed command center, but rather this was more on the level of operational cloak and dagger stuff you read about in a Tom Clancy book.

The pieces fell into place. The directors were both involved in human intelligence programs. The check list and training weren't just to learn how to read a map; it was as tactical as you can get. The identity makeovers and massive amounts of paper work that I had to sign were all signs that this was not just another program. I was getting curious about where I would be assigned and what I was going to collect and report on. One surprise that I did not foresee was the deliberate cold shoulder that I would get in the train stations traveling throughout the DC area. I would see or run into many of these same people that would get me set up and accomplish my tasking. I would try to greet them and have outside conversation with them only to learn that they gave me the cold shoulder and acted like they didn't know me.

I was finally told by Jefferies, who must have heard from someone, that I was being too friendly in the open. Jefferies explained to me that there are many facets to the intelligence agencies and there are always entities tracking, shadowing and monitoring personnel traveling throughout the DC area. He explained that after working for this program, I wouldn't be allowed to come back in the DC area for at least six months. Then he handed me another paper to sign.

The training and preparation was complete. I had only one item left and that was to draw gear. This would be an indicator of where I was going. I was given a list of items to retrieve and directed to go to a commercial, agency-friendly outdoorsmen shop. I was told to keep the shopping down to $3,000.00. I was given a name of a person to see and he would take my shopping list and help me get whatever I needed. Once I got to the place in the DC area, I realized it was a very popular high-end mountain gear shop. The guy took my list, pulled a code off, and told me, "You need to shop for extreme weather conditions." What the heck, I thought I was going to the Iraqi desert. Instead I was heading to some cold mountainous region. I asked him if he could tell me where I was going. He replied, "Nope, but most of the guys that have been drawing this type of gear head to the eastern mountains of Afghanistan." As he told me, he had a silent pause and just looked at me as if he wanted me to get what he was saying so that he could move on to help me with the gear. Back at DIA, Col. Jefferies let the cat out of the bag when he handed me airline tickets and told me who I needed to report to.

It indeed was Afghanistan, and I would end up in the south region known as Kandahar, the birthplace of the Taliban. I would be an agency asset working with 7th Special Forces Group as an intel embed. It was a common procedure to have either a CIA or DIA asset working with the operators while they conducted operations. This was for two primary reasons: one, we were there to help drive future operations and two, the agency wanted their name on any and all findings. This showed Congress and Senate committees that we were good and needed more money to operate. The 7th and 3rd Special Forces Groups were assigned as the counter insurgency specialist in theater. They would rotate in and out of Afghanistan for the next several years as the special operation arm of the war on terror.

USS Midway & USS Missouri (The Mighty Mo) undergoing a log-rep

Snoopy Team pose over the flight deck

Maritime Arms Carrier

Russian Frigate - Udaloy

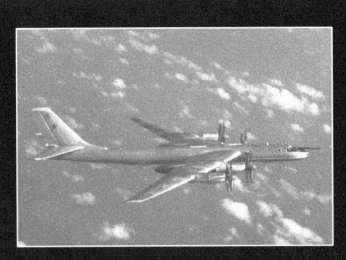

Russian Bear Bomber

Refugee Boat in the Philippine Sea

Mother, twin brother & oldest sister

Twin brother & little sister
at Lake Murray, SC

Amy at old homestead

Before shipping out to Navy

Wedding - July 26, 1986

On a Malibu Beach

Kids in Hawaii - 1999

With family in Hawaii - 2000

Heading out to Afghanistan

Afghanistan near Torkham Gate
Near the Kyber Pass Summit

At Tarnak Farms – UBL's ops

UBL Compound with SSE
collection

Captured AQ flag

AQ Training Compound

AQ first Ops Compound after carpet bombing

In front of an old Russian MIG fighter jet

Afghanistan with an ANA

Raising the Flag at Taliban's last HQ in Kandahar

SSE Collection: RPG Trike in Iraq

SSE Collection: RPG Trike in Iraq

Welcome Home note from my daughter after
almost 8 years of assignments

On the Tail of the Dragon

Blake and I heading out across America

Pit stop going across America with Blake

With Pastor Brad Lambert of Calvary Chapel
Living Hope at Ocean Side Beach

Pastor Dean Ishiki and Will in China Town, SF

Connecting with Victor Marx

Daughter serving at a special needs orphanage
in Mexico

Christian on patrol in an AF village

Friday Morning Bible Study with
Robby Russell

This was one of those "get me" moments,
traveling back from California

Tom Atema of the Heart for Lebanon Organization &
I at the Red Rhino providing a "Tom Talk" on the
topic "Is there Hope for the Middle East?"

With Heart For Lebanon in one of the Syrian
refugee camps in the South

With the Heart For Lebanon organization in one
of the Syrian refugee camps in the Bakaa

With the Heart for Lebanon organization in one
of their H.O.P.E schools in Beirut

Center of Beruit with Amy

With the Heart for Lebanon organization at a
Bedouin Gypsy refugee camp

Elizabeth with Dad

Christian & Blake with Dad

Christian in US Army

Blake in USMC

The kids

Kevin & Liz

With the Family 2016

Chapter 11

HEROES

You could taste the dust in the cold December air. Sargent Collins was yelling through the ranks of people and chaos. "TIG! TIG, where are you!? It was the pitch of night; several people were coordinating different efforts all at the same time. Others where adjusting and fiddling with their night vision goggles. I was about 25 feet away chatting with a couple of EOD dog handlers. I yelled out, "TIG, right over here!" Sergeant Collins began to make his approach to me while also beginning to talk, "TIG, there you are. Sir, you understand that you will be on the second bird, right?" "Roger that, Sarge," I asked for a run-down of the operation and contingency if something were to go wrong. The Sergeant went straight into our op plan without having to even think about it. "Sir, we have 45 minutes on the ground. Once the assault bird arrives and secures the compound, my team will set a perimeter around the area, as well as marshal all the military aged males and persons of interest (POI) in one area, women and children will be marshaled in another area. We will give the ok for the bird you'll be on to make its approach. Sir, once you are on the ground, you will have 30 minutes to do what you do. When I come back around and call out to shut it down, regardless of where you are or what you are doing, you make your way to your bird. Once we get the count secure, then chalks are up. Sir, in the event that we run into some haji magic, we will abort your bird and it will turn back to base and we will convene at the TOC (Tactical Operations Center) for debriefing."

This was a normal night before an operation went down. It was a pre-op run-thru. We would spend about four plus hours going through our 45-minute operation and call it a night. We began earlier in the day by going over a classified targeting meeting and then discussing all the intel on the objective we were getting ready to perform. The who, what, and whys of our target. These operators were good, very good, at what they did. They only want to know exactly what needs to be known, nothing more and definitely nothing less. Too much information would bog them down and too little information could be detrimental. TIG stood for, "The Intel Guy." When in a combat environment, especially on a SOF compound, we had acronyms for most of us guys. Although my title as TIG was a little more personified, other titles for the operators were less personal. For example, some guys would jokingly say, "You are a FAG," which meant that he was a "Former Action Guy." CAG meant that he was a "Current Action Guy." It was a way for us to decipher who was going to be on an objective. FAGs would remain back at the TOC running the operations and providing support in the rear, while the CAG's would be gearing up and preforming the ops.

This was our normal Operational Tempo (Op-tempo), day in and day out. We were always planning the next target, planning the next objective, conducting a pre-op exercise, fine tuning data and plans. Many of these targets were considered HVT's (High Value Targets), later to be known as High Value Individuals and finally POI's. Others were just low level targets. In five months, we would conduct 82 successful operations and have two or three failed objectives. They were not without a cost though. We had several losses and had several near misses.

On January 5, 2005 SFC Pedro Munoz and his team were conducting an objective to capture a mid-level Taliban commander in the Shindad region in western Afghanistan. The operation immediately went from non-kinetic to kinetic. As the team was clearing a room on the compound, a POI fired off several rounds in the room filled with women and children in an attempt to barricade himself or shield himself from the SOF team. SFC Munoz was hit immediately but was able to reposition himself, shielding his team from harm and selectively firing off counter rounds to take out the combatant and other hostiles while also ensuring no women and children were hit. This allowed the rest of the team to continue with the operation and clear the compound. SFC Munoz later died from

132

complications of taking on enemy fire. Left behind were his wife and daughter who was only about 11 or 12 years old.

That night was purely a future motivator. We were never more motivated after that to find any and every piece of "actionable intelligence" we could to continue our campaign of sweeping up Taliban and al-Qaeda members in the Kandahar Valley.

Two days later we stood outside of our compound in ranks and had a ceremony for our fallen warrior. It was one of the saddest moments of my entire life. Additionally, I observed most of the SOF Operators break down their rough, solid exterior and cry over the loss of their teammate. These men were the elite of the entire Army, yet they all showed a soft side. As the chaplain came up to share some words of comfort, I kept thinking what a horrific scene before me of SFC Munoz's belongings (his combat boots, beret, dog-tags and M-4) grouped together behind a picture of him, and displayed up in front of all these soldiers who were standing at parade rest. After the chaplain spoke and prayed, each soldier went up and paid their respects their own way. Some would lay down their highest medal awards earned.

Part of me was definitely saddened, but another part of me was very proud to be there doing what I was doing. I was just in awe of the moment. Frankly, I was privileged to be there supporting such an important period in time. Most do not know the cost and sacrifices these men must make to keep our country and others, including those that despise our initiatives, safe.

My shop became a hub for members of Munoz's team to visit and press me for any information I could find to link them to the next target. Again, the motivator was heightened. It was not long after that objective that I found myself on a different type of collection mission. Instead of being on a combat detail, myself and several others were on a combined covert mission to collect information for an upcoming objective. We had to travel into Kandahar to meet up with a group of South Africans who had key information we needed. The South Africans were hired to come into the country and help sweep for mines. Their ability to be in forbidden locations was a plus for us as they would come in contact with locals which produced conversations of value, which is what we were after. The problem was not getting into the city and navigating through the multitudes of people in broad daylight, but rather getting out and back to base without being noticed. That was always the hard part.

The afternoon of this mission, we drove into Kandahar and pulled into a gated safe house where we put on female burkas. These were long indigenous dresses with full head covering, only leaving a meshed see-through area for the eyes. It was a perfect cover to travel and walk about in the city to be incognito. They were also large enough to allow us to carry our weapons underneath if we ended up getting into a conflict. We had to have a quick lesson to walk differently and learn how to stop and look around. We could stand anywhere and listen to conversations all day long, virtually un-noticed. We had a local source with us who helped us navigate to places we needed to be. On this day, I would have a SAS British soldier with me and two British SOCA agents. SAS was the Special Air Service. They were the British version of our Special Forces. The SOCA agency is Combined MI-5 and British Custom Agency. SOCA stands for Serious Organized Crime Agency. They would be like our FBI, yet on steroids. One of the SOCA agents would go as he was with our local source and the rest of us incognito and follow along at a very loose pace in the distance. After he would conclude his conversations and leave, we would move to a nearby table to sit and listen, allowing us collect what was said after the initial make.

It was pitch-black, no street lights, on a one-lane road covered by rigid mountains that camouflaged Taliban extremists. Myself, a SAS soldier, and two British SOCA agents were speeding down Highway 1 to get back to Kandahar Airfield. Suddenly, two unidentified cars came up on us. How were we marked? During the day time, the Afghan police had check points set up throughout the city to present a presence of safety. At night, though, it was a different story. The Afghan police were as corrupt as you can get. They would take bribes from the Taliban to have one of their insiders at the check points to report any unusual activity. We were coming through at night in a large SUV which was unusual. At the first, second and third check point we were fine. However, once we passed through the fourth check point, we were marked and being followed, which turned into a high-speed chase down Highway 1. We drove right through check point five almost running over the person there in an attempt to get away from the vehicle that was chasing us, but it only caused them to grab another vehicle and join in the chase.

Two cars chasing us with eight miles to go seemed like an eternity. There were bounty prices on our heads if they found out we were intelligence personnel. To have one of us would have been bad enough, but all three of us from different intelligence organizations would be a massive leverage, if not a national security issue on a global scale. Getting captured was not an option. So, with the gun pressing up against the window, I had the laser grips of my Sig Sauer hand gun squeezed as tight as I could, all the while crossing over Gordy our driver, causing him to look up and over my arms. The laser dot set its target on the head of the passenger holding his AK-47 out of the white truck next to us. I was screaming at the top of my lungs, "Back off or I will put a bullet through your head!" Whether it was the laser dot on the leader's head or my persuasive words, the truck beside us backed off, the car in front of us moved out of the way and we were full throttle back to base. Attempting to regain some normal composure, Gordy lightened things up and said, "Thank you! Good God man! They are messing with the wrong sailor!" We all chuckled and took a few deeper breaths to recompose ourselves. I would never forget the phrase and would use it jokingly when wrestling with my kids later in life.

Many other events, issues and concerns took place over the next few months. The Op-tempo began to pick up due to some credible intelligence we were able to pull from previous objectives. Along with increased mission requirements came regular attacks from the Taliban. More corruption infiltrated the ranks of our operations. The Afghan National Police were also being corrupted. Police officers were not showing up for work and were known to take bribes. The Afghan National Army was doing the same. The trust meter was leaning more to the left. Uniforms and people were missing which made it harder and harder to achieve our objectives. We had to have the support of the local population in order to help stabilize the country. I recall at least two objectives we pursued that went dark. We came back with zero because the targets were tipped off early.

135

On another occasion, we flew out to an objective, dropped down the bird for a capture/kill operation and squatters took off from the target compound for the hills. There was no way to completely secure the facility. Upon departure from the objective, there was to be a count of individuals back on the helo, just as there was when they come off the helo before the beginning of the operation. At this particular objective, the crew master did not count, or miscounted, the assault team exfilling the objective. He only had 11 and not 12. One was left behind. What made it worse was no one knew it until an hour later after getting back to the TOC to do a debrief. Sargent Lentz was left behind in hostile territory with limited ammo, no food, no comms, and 23 miles from post. All that was on him was a tracking device.

As I walked in the TOC to provide the commander some intelligence that was found from the objective, I realized I walked into a hail storm. The commander was firm, yet refrained from yelling, and asked, "What happened, and where is Sargent Lentz! Are we trying to locate him?" He immediately turned to me and said, "We are canceling this brief tonight. If you can, find me anything that would help us locate Lentz." He then turned to the FBI assets we had on post and told them to do the same. Within a few minutes, the commander had the entire TOC engaged to find Lentz. Some were on the COMs with NSA to help ping the tracker. Others were pulling maps up to reverse the navigation and assess where Lentz may be traveling. It seemed like pure chaos, but it was actually accurate delegation. I left the TOC and went back down to my shop to see if there was anything else I could find. Several hours passed by the time I went back up to the TOC to update the commander with nothing. I walked in and Jax, one of the FBI agents embedded there, told me that Sargent Lentz was on foot trying to get back to our post. He was about seven miles out. The commander launched a helo to go find and pick him up. The rescue helo did find him on the outskirts of a nearby village and retrieved him. While picking him up, they dropped a crypto device by accident out of the helo and were unable to find it. It was a night of nail-biting drama. Sargent Lentz came into the TOC screaming. He walked up to the crew master yelling at the top of his lungs. "Were you trying to get me killed!" Lentz was ok, the crew master was fired and re-assigned, and operations continued.

The days seemed to be getting longer; the nights were being interrupted by mortar rounds popping. Anxiety was heightened, the work was getting harder, and the Taliban was getting smarter as were al-Qaeda members. I was beginning to ask myself if it was worth it or not. It felt like each operation would take little bit of my soul. I happened to run into someone that began to help me see the light at the end of the tunnel. Well, I should say, he ran into me. He showed up at my shop in need of some information from some documents in a folder we found in a compound that had explosives and IED material. It was a training manual off one of the targets we were chasing. Les was working for the Joint Improvised Explosive Defeat Organization (JIEDO) as a defense contractor. He and I began to collaborate on each other's work, and I ended up letting him use a space in my office any time he needed it. I felt it was important to further other's efforts to accomplish their goals because one day they may end up saving my life. The environment we worked in was a very ego-driven environment and one has to fight to be above it. Much of the ego was the result of having to face the possibility of one day dying on the battlefield. Les was a former SOF operator. He spent most of his time in 10th and 5th groups and running operations in Europe. He knew the game and trials I was facing and began to help take away the strain of trying to accomplish so much for what I was assigned to do. He encouraged me to run with him at least once a week and hang out with him on Tuesday nights to smoke cigars over at the Air Force compound not far from where we were working. Without knowing it, he was able to level me out and educate me on how these operators worked and how I need to respond to them and them to me. Additionally, Les had a spiritual side to him that attracted my attention. I was so far off the grid walking with God that I just didn't know where to pick up again. He wasn't overly spiritual about things, but he did believe in God and made it known in a natural way. It was something that I respected about him; he made me re-think my position with my Creator. I have always been grateful for him coming into my life when he did. Due to the uncertainty of hostile chaos around me coupled with the fact that I had been on the run from God since I thought I failed at planting a Calvary Chapel in the Appalachian Mountains, Les was a God-send.

Les was a highly decorated veteran who spent time in the Gulf due to his familiarity with the Arabic language, as well as in Berlin during the Cold War. His unit was part of a contingency which was a stay-behind unit that monitored and helped prevent future Soviet occupation in Germany. This force dated as far back as the 1950s. Their unit was a highly classified detachment known as "Alpha Teams." A-team would be comprised of five specialized operators and one captain. They were spread throughout Germany and then greater Europe. Les was not only a special operator, he was also a certified Army diver who understood explosives, and was one of the Army's foremost skilled snipers. These operators were not just your normal solider. They were soldiers on steroids. They worked very closely with the CIA and other foreign intelligence entities. While in Berlin, he and his team conducted clandestine snatch-and-grab operations. His unit was also there when the Berlin Wall came down.

Les would not only help me to refocus my perspective, he would help me by introducing me to other operators that were able to drop their egos and be real men without the hero status. These guys began to help me reshape the meaning of life, reminding me that God is real, evil does exist, and men are called to prevail against it. When put in those terms, life became easier. This war in Afghanistan only proved to me that God existed because evil existed. I remember one day Les introduced me to a friend of his that I yielded a great deal of respect for. When introduced, Les said, "Will, this is Tony... better known as Bucket." They began to catch up on who was where and who we lost. A moment of soberness quickly turned into a chuckle as they began to talk about some memorable moments.

Les began to tell me the story of when they were training Jordanian Commandos at a U.S. training location. One morning six of the commandos did not show up for their training session. Les sent one of his soldiers to look for them. The soldier came back and reported to Les that something terrible had happened. The guys did not answer their dorm door and blood was all over the side walk leading up to the dorm. Les and his team took off to assess the situation. As they got to the dorms, they noticed a long trail of blood from the road onto the sidewalk leading up to the dorm. All Les could think about was this major international crime incident with special forces and foreign delegates. He only saw Leavenworth bars before his eyes; he was responsible for these guys. Les knocked on the door several times before kicking it open. As he entered the room, he saw nothing but large amounts of blood all over the place leading into the bedroom. Once he entered, he saw the sheets on the bed soaked in blood. His own blood-pressure dropped, and he turned white in the face as he noticed a trail of blood leading into the bathroom. What happened next shocked him. He opened the door and found three of the Jordanian Commandos leaning over the bathtub skinning a deer. He asked, "What the hell is going on here?" Just as he said that, the other three commandos came walking through the door with beer and a bag of charcoal chips. He turned back to the others in the bathtub and yelled, "What are you guys doing?" The commandos said, "We are going to have a bar-b-que Master Sargent. Join us. Join us!" The story is, they were coming home from a late-night tour of the town and hit a deer on the road. Instead of leaving it there, they brought it back to the dorm to skin and cook it. Les stated that it took him all day and some very clever convincing to keep all this under cover.

Another story I recall is when Bucket was recruited to the Special Operations Forces. It was Les that had to interview him to be on his team. Selection for SOF teams was like going through a gauntlet. It was not easy and the entry rate was 1 in 10. A person really had to impress these team leaders to be on their team. Les and Bucket were laughing about how Bucket was recruited. All the recruits had to come before the team leaders and give a presentation of their skills and why they should be a SOF operator on the team for which they were applying. Bucket was different. He did something no one else had ever done before or since. Most guys would share how well they did in the "Q" course (qualifying course to be a special force operator). They would brag about their excellent marksmanship, how well they knew their equipment list, what guns and arms they were familiar with, and what languages they could speak. Every recruit came in doing the same routine, except Bucket.

When Les called in the next potential team member, a large barrel-chested man came in with shoulders as wide as he was tall and on top of those shoulders stood a head with very little neck. (Hence the name Bucket was coined). Les asked him, "Why do you want to be on my team, and why should I hire you?" Bucket spoke up as sweat was beading all around his face and head and said, "Master Sargent, my name is Tony Pryor. I am from Oregon, and I have a few show-and-tell items that I want to present which might answer your questions." Tony then stepped out of the room and rolled in a couple of carts of tree gear and began to set up.

After about 15 minutes or so, Tony had built a display of chainsaws of all shapes and sizes and pictures of enormous trees as well as cut out tree rings. Les was actually in awe of this guy. Tony "Bucket" Pryor grabbed a large chainsaw with a long 30-inch blade on it and ripped the cord to start it up. He began to yell over the sound of the saw briefing Master Sargent on the importance of using the right tool for the right job. He continued to go through several other sizes of saws showing how to properly handle each one safely. Les stated that this guy showed more muscles than he had ever seen, from his bucket head down to his arms. Tony then showed him a canvas of pictures of how he and his brothers would haul trees. Master Sargent noticed in the pictures that Bucket carried portions of tree trunks that seemed beyond the ability of a normal man to carry. He thought, "This guy is an animal." Les and his other leaders just stood in the room with their mouths dropped down to the floor in awe. Bucket turned around with great humility and stated, "Sir, this is who I am. I am from Oregon, and I come from a family of lumberjacks. I love what I do, I love my country, and I want to serve it. I will do whatever it takes, but this is who I am. Take it or leave it.

Needless to say, Les hired him on his team, and it was a good thing. Bucket became one of his best teammates. Although very quiet and humble, he was noted amongst his teammates as one of the bravest operators they had. He helped other team members cope with the stress of combat operations. Bucket became the subject of a news article during one of his operations just a couple of years before. I could not resist finding this article and including it, as reporter Gregg Zoroya got more of an inside glimpse of Tony.

USA Today

October 20, 2003

Inches Divide Life, Death In The Afghan Darkness

By Gregg Zoroya, USA Today

For a few seconds on a frigid Afghan night, Army Master Sgt. Tony Pryor fought America's war on terror with only his bare hands.

One of 26 Special Forces soldiers raiding an al-Qaeda compound in mountains north of Kandahar last year, Pryor found himself alone in a room with three enemy fighters. He shot two of them dead in the first few seconds. The third he would have to fight — and kill — hand to hand, so close he could smell the man's sour breath.

War creates widows, orphans, disabled Purple Heart veterans — and soldiers such as Pryor, proficient in the dark art of killing. All of the nation's nearly 30,000 special operations soldiers, sailors and airmen are skilled at close combat. But Pryor was specially trained. He was one of more than 80 Army Special Forces troops who drilled relentlessly in close-quarter fighting — a combination of martial arts and street fighting — to prepare for a series of raids in Afghanistan.

"Whatever digging, scratching, biting, hair-pulling, ear-ripping-off — whatever you got to do to get the job done, that's what you do," Pryor says, explaining actions that night that won him the Silver Star for heroism and saved the lives of other team members in the compound. "Because, bottom line, I got a life at home. They (his comrades) got a life at home. And we're coming home."

That kind of close-up killing, though rare in Afghanistan, has become more common in the broader fighting of Iraq. In several fights, including the attack on the 507th Maintenance Company in which Pfc. Jessica Lynch was captured, American soldiers have been required to fight and kill Iraqis face-to-face.

It is killing not from the more sterile distance of a cruise missile launch or tank turret but so near the enemy that the soldiers sometimes hear the rattle of a last breath.

"Not nice business," Pryor says grimly.

The specific reason for the assault that night remains a secret. The soldiers say only that they were after intelligence on al-Qaeda and that the raid was a success. The fight for the compound lasted 20 minutes. But it was the most intense clash any of the Green Beret soldiers had experienced.

In a recent interview at 5th Special Forces Group headquarters at Fort Campbell, Ky., Pryor describes fighting and dying that was nothing like the slick Hollywood portrayal in action films.

A 40-year-old father, Pryor asks this reporter to turn off a tape recorder before he recounts the most graphic details of his hand-to-hand struggle.

"Would you want your kid to know that about you?" he then asks.

This is his story.

Epitome of a warrior

On Jan. 22, 2002, as Pryor and the other Special Forces soldiers prepared to helicopter into the mountains north of Kandahar, they paused for a prayer at base camp. Sgt. 1st Class James Hogg asked God to fill their hearts with courage. Pryor wore a medallion of St. Michael, the patron saint of soldiers, duct-taped to his dog tag.

The men were "direct action" A-Team members, also known as assaulters, door-kickers or "five-minute wonders." They are the first to enter buildings, and they use SWAT team-like tactics. Close-in combat skills are crucial.

Pryor, the senior enlisted officer that night, is a bull of a man. Only 5-foot-11, he weighs 235 pounds. At the time, he could bench-press almost twice that. Team members call him a ferocious competitor, the epitome of a warrior.

"He makes you a better soldier just being around him," says Sgt. 1st Class Steve Ourada, a team member. "He built that assault force into what it was. We were on top of our game."

From aerial photos, their target looked like a U-shaped building within a walled compound. But on the ground that night, they found it was actually three buildings separated by covered breezeways.

The team charged into one breezeway and lobbed a flash-bang grenade, designed to disorient enemy troops, into the central courtyard. The area was filled with shiny new Toyota pickups and a trailer carrying a dual-barreled anti-aircraft weapon. Al-Qaeda fighters fired back, and the bullets raised clouds of stone from walls of the alleyway.

The troops had to push through the gunfire and cut left and right to clear rooms. Pryor, whose healthy-size cranium has earned him the nickname "Bucket," led the way. He stepped around a corner and shot a man coming at him with an AK-47 a few feet away.

Night-vision goggles cast everything in a greenish hue and gave the Special Forces troops an advantage. Al-Qaeda fighters, most of them bearded men wearing long dishdashas, floor-length shirts, had only the starlight.

Even so, the al-Qaeda men appeared well-trained and disciplined. Twenty-one of them would fight to the death.

Close-quarters battle

As Pryor entered the first room to his right, he came face-to-face with a second fighter emerging from the doorway. Unable to see a weapon in that split-second, Pryor slugged the man and knocked him down, blowing past him into the room. But the fighter rose with an AK-47. Hogg, still in the courtyard, fired a single round from his M-4 carbine and killed the man.

Other team members had gone on to clear the rest of the buildings, and Pryor faced the fighters in the room alone. If any got past him — or worse, killed Pryor — they could shoot other GIs in the back.

It was Pryor's fight now to win. As he entered the 25-by-25-foot room, his eyes swept from left to right. Bedrolls littered the floor, and two fighters at the rear of the room took aim through windows at other Americans entering the compound. Both swung toward Pryor, Kalashnikovs in their hands. Pryor fired, the rounds striking so dead-center that the men's beards fluttered.

As he reloaded, Pryor felt a foot brush up against his boot. At first, he thought it was another American. It wasn't. An al-Qaeda fighter struck Pryor hard from behind. The blow, possibly from a wooden board, dislocated Pryor's shoulder and broke his collarbone.

The fighter, bearded with his hair in a ponytail, jumped on Pryor's back and clawed at his face, tearing off his night-vision goggles.

"He started sticking his stinking little fingers into my eyeballs," Pryor remembers.

His left shoulder felt like it was on fire. He was winded and weary from fighting at an altitude of 8,000 feet. Without night vision, everything was black.

The battle outside raged on, punctuated by AK-47 and rifle fire and the steady boom of a 40mm grenade launcher from a Special Forces Humvee. The air reeked of gunpowder and the copper scent of blood. Inside that first room, the two fighters — al-Qaeda and American — were fighting to the death.

Pryor had only a single thought: You're not going to kill me.

"That's how I attack things," he says later.

With one good arm, Pryor grabbed his enemy by the hair. But the man's weight, combined with the 80 pounds of Army gear that Pryor wore, caused the two to fall. They landed on Pryor's left elbow, and the impact jammed his shoulder back into its socket.

Now he could fight with both hands. In a few desperate seconds, Pryor broke the man's neck and finished him with a 9mm pistol.

Miraculously, not another American was injured that night.

"There aren't any widows or orphans because of him," Ourada says of Pryor.

'They'd aged about 10 years'

In his 14 years in the Special Forces, Pryor has killed before, but never in hand-to-hand fighting. That night, he worried first, however, about his soldiers, who had shot it out with al-Qaeda inside other rooms.

Around a wood fire at base camp hours later, Pryor offered solace. "I went around and touched every one of those guys," he says. "Everybody looked like they'd aged about 10 years."

For him, sleepless nights followed.

He dispelled demons with cathartic heart-to-heart talks with his tentmate Hogg, replaying details of the fighting and dying. "A little bit of defragging of your hard drive," Pryor calls it.

Three articles of faith got him through, he says.

First was pride in a successful mission: Training had paid off.

Second was seeing the war as righteous. "We didn't start it," Pryor says. "They started this fight. We're in the right."

Third was his children and the future. "I remember him saying," Hogg recalls, " 'You know, it's an ugly business, it's a terrible thing for us to do. But hopefully our kids won't have to cope with it.' "

In addition to Pryor's Silver Star, seven Green Berets in the unit received Bronze Stars for valor in that fight. Pryor sent letters to their fathers. "I would like to thank you for raising a fine young man," he wrote. Many of the letters wound up framed and hung in living rooms.

Including Pryor, 19 soldiers have received the nation's third-highest decoration for fighting in Afghanistan. One soldier received the second-highest award, the Distinguished Service Cross.

This year, 86 additional Silver Stars were awarded by the Army for fighting in Operation Iraqi Freedom. And one Army engineer, Sgt. 1st Class Paul Ray Smith, made a last stand with a .50-caliber machinegun against dozens of attacking Iraqi soldiers during fighting in April at the international airport outside Baghdad. He is being considered posthumously for the Medal of Honor, the military's highest decoration.

'No idea of the toll it takes'

"The thing that kind of boggles my mind," says James Bradley, author of Flags of Our Fathers, the story of the fighting and flag-raising on Iwo Jima during World War II, "is that (the nation is) sending out these guys who would rather be whittling and spending time with their kids. And they're sending them out to kill. They have no idea of the toll it takes on humans to do something like that."

Maj. Gen. Geoff Lambert, a former Special Forces commander, agrees.

"In all wars, there are certain circumstances like this that happen to good men," Lambert says. "We try to train them the best we can to have them ready for these moments. We hope that they are few."

To cope with killing, Pryor says he lives two lives: one consumed with training for and fighting war, the other immersed in family.

"Two different lifestyles, two different on-and-off switches," he says. "If you're Johnny on the spot, focused on destruction, destruction, destruction all the time, where do you have time for compassion in a relationship with your wife? We're dedicated to our job. But there has to be a time to turn that off."

It is not easy for him to explain how he flips this switch, though he says that one way is to simply not discuss work and war when he leaves the base.

It bothers him that civilians might see him and his troops as Rambo-like soldiers.

"People look at people who do this stuff and it's always, 'They're killers, and that's what they live for,' " Pryor says. "That is so far from the reality."

Certainly, they don't shrink from the task of taking life if necessary. Pryor is a student of Sun Tzu's classic The Art of War, and a favorite topic is the legend of the Mongoday, the elite warriors of Genghis Khan. He and his troops train exhaustively in spotting the enemy and withholding fire.

The night of the assault, members of a farming family armed with a rifle in a building that was searched nearby were left untouched because they offered no resistance. And at the height of action, with adrenaline raging, an al-Qaeda fighter chose to surrender and was taken unharmed.

The control seems as ingrained as the reaction.

The other GIs tell of a firefight weeks earlier during which Pryor entered a room that was ablaze and spotted movement under a blanket. He didn't shoot. Pausing to search, he found a baby girl, pulled her free and passed her to a team member.

Off the battlefield, Pryor has a gentle reputation. For security reasons, he declines to discuss immediate family, but he says he forbids toy guns in his home.

Ourada remembers finding "Bucket" in his garage once nursing a newborn raccoon with an eye dropper. "The wives just think he's a big old teddy bear," Hogg says.

'It never goes away'

Raised in the logging town of Toledo, Ore., Pryor grew up admiring perseverance and hard work. A strong influence was his father, Jerry Pryor, who started out as a timber man and became the town chief of police.

The first movie Pryor saw in a theater was The Green Berets with John Wayne. He says the image of these soldiers stayed with him when he enlisted in the Army out of high school in 1981.

Though he was earning straight A's by the end of high school, college held no appeal. Like other young men from rural towns, he longed to escape. In 1988, he was accepted into the Green Berets, one of 79 chosen from an entry class of 429.

He has been on missions in Haiti, Somalia, Kuwait and other locations that remain classified. Early this year, he led a team in Iraq. Next year, he

147

attends the Army's Sergeants Major Academy at Fort Bliss, Texas, on track to attain the highest enlisted rank.

He has also started working toward a business degree. After retiring from the Army, perhaps in three years, he hopes one day to manage a sawmill.

He has had two reconstructive surgeries to repair damage from that battle in Afghanistan. A chunk of his collarbone, removed during an operation, is kept in a jar as a souvenir. That, and the violent images, are what he has left.

"It never goes away," Pryor says. "It just gets put further back in your mind."

Hogg, the teammate who helped Pryor exorcise his demons from that night, says these are the prices they pay for lethal work.

"I wouldn't wish it on anybody," Hogg says. "But there are a few of us who are called to it. So that's what we do. Maybe people should at least keep us in their prayers."

These men became my brothers. They not only knew the art and evil of war, but they also knew the importance of laughing off the bad moments and thanking God for each and every breath they took. Although I did not have to go through half of what they went through because I was just an intel embed helping them with sensitive site exploitation, I did learn a great deal about being a silent, brave warrior that always remains humble and never lets fear grip the call of courage.

"Tactics, Techniques, and Procedures" became a buzz phrase within our compound. The operators were looking to my shop to help them understand what the tactics of the enemy were, what techniques they were using, and what common procedures they used to accomplish their attacks. Over the last remaining months in Kandahar, I was able to outline a pattern of life for how the members of the Taliban operated and how the elements of al-Qaeda used media techniques to misinform coalition forces. I began to collaborate with the HUMINT shop to exchange information which would be used to resource foreign assets to collect additional information and draw us closer to the extremists.

Still struggling with the stress of it all, we identified over 82 targets or POI's and neutralized them. Several weeks before I left, I was involved in writing a white paper and technical report to the Defense Intelligence Agency on the use of intelligence operators in combat. I received a call from one of our HUMINT personal. They asked me to come with them and bring my interpreter to help with an asset we were developing. After a couple of hours, we put all the pieces together and moved our asset back into place, which would take several days. The information gained from this was not only credible, but highly sensitive. I had never been in a situation where I had to make a decision to hold onto information that should be reported but could not be reported at the exact time we received it. I made an agreement with the HUMINT officer that I would hold on to the report for two days before releasing it through national channels. When the third day came and the report was released, all hell broke loose.

It was mid-June, and I got a call from CJTF (Combine Joint Task Force) up in Bagram, where they were headquartered. It was Col. Jackson. He asked if I could go on a secure line. He began to ask about the report and wanted to know why I held onto it for two days and didn't push it out. He said, "Don't you think this information is important? Damn it Will, you have the first bit of intelligence on Bin Laden's possible location and what tribe in Pakistan he is hiding out with. Don't you think that is of national importance!" Col. Jackson continued to give me the third degree and demanded that I come up and face the General of CJTF to explain why I held on to such important information. I finally interrupted the Col. and told him that I couldn't come up, I had to fly out to CONUS in a few days to get back to DIA for a debrief. The Colonel demanded my arrival within the next few hours. I finally laid it out for him. I said, "Sir, this was a need-to-know operation involving a SOF unit infilling and exfilling a highly sensitive asset across international boundaries into territory that was both astir and hostile. Releasing this information too early would have possibly gotten him killed and compromised my operator's objective, putting them in harm's way. Not to mention, it would also have jeopardized future collection efforts."

I could tell that Col. Jackson was not pleased, yet he noted back to me that it was a difficult situation to be placed. Frustrating as it was, he now had enough information to go on, and I needed to work on getting my flight back out to DIA. He later called me before leaving the country to tell me how proud he was to have me on his team. He also wrote my oldest son a letter to tell him about my great exploits. It was the first time in several months that Usama bin Laden was reported on and the information would be one of the first and most crucial pieces of a puzzle which would ultimately lead to UBL's capture and demise.

The coming days were like a stock chart with up moments and down moments. I had to figure out how to get back to DC on a timely note. It was easy to get into the country, but very hard to get a flight out. There were days I had a flight out only to be canceled by bad weather or other problems. I ended up picking up a flight to Germany at about 3:00am. It was a special flight with a special passenger, and it was the highlight of my entire assignment. He and I became the closest friends in the eight-hour flight to Frankfurt. He did not say one thing to me, but I knew that he had put in a good tour. I was encouraged and felt more safe than I have ever felt before with him being there and being on the front lines. He sat in the middle of the C17, and I was on the side looking right at him. He never left my eyes for eight hours. And although he said nothing, he spoke to me and filled my heart with a great sense of accomplishment, yet his was even greater. I knew that his parents would be proud of him and all his buddies in the unit would be grateful for the work he had done. If he had kids, I knew that they would be very proud of him also. I remember at one point I was so tired after being up some 20+ hours that I had to lay down on the steel girders and try to get some sleep. My friend had no problem with me lying next to him. I fell asleep for about an hour and awoke to find him in the same position. I awoke with my eyes still fixed on him and still in great awe of how my tour was ending with me being in his presence. He was sharply dressed in the American uniform appropriate for one ending his tour. I could not help but stare at his handsome attire. I was touched as the

C17 landed and all crew got off except he and I. I wanted to say something but could not, as he had many people come on board and began escorting him off. All I could do is render a salute and say thank you for my freedom. Again, he said nothing, but I sense he would have said, "You're welcome," by how he wore his departing uniform. I never got his name, and I will not forget what he looked like. He looked like a great hero to me and that is what I will call him. Six finely dressed soldiers picked him up, straightened his uniform, he was wearing the American flag, and carried him off. He was a KIA, the 3rd one I was somehow affiliated with, and his name was Hero.

Chapter 11 is dedicated to operators and warriors who have sacrificed greatly for the liberty of others. Remember them and know that it comes at a great cost.

"Bad things happen, when good men stand by and do nothing."

The war in Afghanistan resulted in approximately 2372 deaths of military operators.
The war in Iraq resulted in approximately 4486 deaths of military operators.

Thank God for these brave men and women who did not stand by and do nothing.

Chapter 12

HONEY-POT

Two months had not gone by when I received another phone call from a small defense contracting firm. Somehow my resume ended up in this firm's office. They asked if I would be interested in a project manager's position. I agreed to an interview in Northern Virginia and ended up being one of two potential hires for the position. The other candidate was better qualified, as it would be a state-side position with travel. They preferred to keep me on and push me to Iraq to work on intelligence collection efforts to find all former Saddam Hussein regime members.

Prior to U.S. invasion and before Saddam's regime fell and he went into hiding, he had ordered one of his sons to go to the Central Bank of Iraq (CBI) and take all the money. There was purportedly 1 billion dollars in cash that was stored in aluminum containers. These containers ended up being divided amongst key members of his regime. They split up and went to find refuge elsewhere, either in other regions of Iraq or in neighboring countries. My new assignment would call for me and other team members to track down these former regime members. Most of them were on the 100 Most Wanted List or what we called the "black list." Most Americans were more familiar with Saddam's deck of cards. These terrorists, war criminals, and dictators were on a deck of cards that were printed out in masses and used to help locate and track them down.

Flying into Iraq was so much different than flying into Afghanistan. Iraq had a certain feel about it. As soon as I stepped off the plane it seemed and felt like there was a curse or omen floating around the air. I thought I was heading over to one of the former dictator's palaces in Bagdad which had been converted into a US and Allied intelligence operations center, but that was not the case. Five of us were being pushed out to a forward operating base (FOB) called Abu Ghraib.

Abu Ghraib was absolutely the last place that I would want to be assigned to. It had a history of evil. The FOB itself was an Iraqi prison that Saddam would use to incarcerate political prisoners. It is reported that he used it as a death camp for those who disagreed with his leadership and more than a thousand people were executed there and buried nearby in mass graves. In the early 2000's Saddam decided to close the prison just prior to US invasion to either use it to show what a great guy he was or to wreak havoc on his nation. Thousands of prisoners were released and the prison doors shut. What many don't realize is that just a short couple of miles down the road was a biological weapons plant that was disguised as a baby milk factory. Saddam's regime went as far as having a sign painted on top of the plant that said, "Baby Formula Plant." There were several of these biological plants around the area at one time.

This area was also known for a scandal of mistreating Iraqi prisoners by US military soldiers. The incident had taken place just a year and a half before I arrived, but was still in the news. Just four months before driving through those gates, the FOB was overrun by extremists. Two suicide bombers penetrated the gates and 80 plus militants came through, shooting Marine guards and other military personnel. The operating task force's commander and her command sergeant were caught hiding in their office under a desk. They were later relieved of duty due to dereliction of duty. Soldiers died that day due to a lack of leadership. Two more attacks would be attempted within days after this overrun. Abu Ghraib was a key target for al-Qaeda in Iraq as it imprisoned several key leaders of al-Zarqawi, Usama bin Laden's right-hand man. Zarqawi called for the attacks in hopes of freeing some of his lieutenants. Abu Ghraib would undergo at least two more major attacks, one of which over 600 prisoners would escape.

As I write this, I realize how fortunate I was to not be caught up in any of those attacks. There were some brave soldiers that paid a price for protecting US interests.

My assignment was to collect and report on valued intelligence gathered from detainees held there. Many of them were al-Qaeda operatives. We had so many captured individuals coming through that it was difficult to keep up with all the information. Some that were detained were what we called "foreign fighters." They were from other countries like Russia, Turkey and Saudi Arabia, as well as others. They were there to fight in the name of Jihad. One particular person of interest was from Russia whom we called the Crazy Russian. He broke away from the crowd, stole a pair of scissors off the sentry's desk, and tried to attack us. The entire detainee population entered into an attitude of revolt and we thought we were going to be overtaken until one of the MP's tackled the Crazy Russian to the ground.

On another occasion, we had multiple "capture or kill" operations going on back to back. We experienced an influx of detainees which made it hard to determine who was who in the zoo. One day after preparing for an interrogation, I was screening collected information off one individual and noted some names and numbers in his ledger. After further research and questioning we were able to deduce that this particular person was an agent or former agent of the Iraqi Intelligence Service (the IIS). They were Saddam's clandestine arm known for many attempted assassinations around the world. This list in his possession was a list of CIA assets we had working on classified objectives. How he got the list and names we don't know, but he did. We later found out that one of the other persons we were detaining was one of our assets, and his name was on that list. We called his handler and were able to get him back out in the field. As for the other guy, we sent him back to Saudi Arabia as a foreign fighter. Saudi Arabia had a strict terrorism law. If caught as a terrorist it was immediate public execution.

There were a lot of crazy things that went on there in Iraq, and in Abu Ghraib. The term "war is hell" began to be defined for me. We were collecting more intelligence than we knew how to handle. I was traveling once a week into Baghdad to meet with US Treasury agents, CIA assets, DIA assets, and US Marshalls. I was also the military and coalition advisor as part of the first Threat Financial Intelligence Group (TFIG). We were using every angle we could to neutralize Saddam's former regime. I was flying to other FOBs, driving on known ambushed roads, being shot at from nearby fields, driving up on the road where IED's were just picked up or blown up hours before. All I had to keep my sanity was working 12 to 14 hours a day and a morning run around the camp. It was a struggle to put all the moving pieces of the puzzle together. Then one day we had a breakthrough. We found some key information which led to a series of successful attacks. This also led to some key persons of interest. One being Abu al-Zarqawi, Iraq's main al-Qaeda leader. Zarqawi was a master-mind of multiple terrorist attacks throughout the Middle East. He ran countless networks in Turkey, Jordan, Iraq, Iran and other places. He was responsible for hotel bombings and killings of US and foreign allies. We were able to find one of his drivers which eventually led to al-Zarqawi's compound. It was a major victory for me and the Task Force.

Not long after, orders came down to close the FOB and move all detainees to Camp Cropper, the new internment facility that held all the key players. Everyone moved out except 13 of us. It was a very freaky feeling to be stuck there at Abu Ghraib with very little fire-power and knowing that it had been attacked multiple times already. For one or two weeks, I lived in constant anxiety believing that death was going to happen any moment. It was a horrible way to operate. Added to this stress were the fearful moments haunting my mind from my time in Afghanistan the year before. I began to believe that I was destined to die in this life that I was living as a field intelligence professional. Every morning I would wake up thinking this was going to be the day. Suicide bombers were going to penetrate the gates again and release the detainees and have all thirteen of us lined up for a YouTube beheading. It may sound far-fetched, but the reality was, it was a real possibility. It had happened before, and I could not shake the feeling that I could die at any moment. I jokingly used the phrase, "I am a dead man walking."

The day came that it was time for us to escort the last remaining detainees on a bus and convoy them an hour into Baghdad to Camp Cropper. We were to pack up the last remaining documents and get the heck out of dodge. Task Force 134 was being allocated to Camp Cropper. We were being assigned to bigger and better things. Saddam Hussein had arrived about the same time we were arriving. Camp Cropper became the internment facility for all the Baath Party members and other High Valued Detainees (HVD). Many AQ operatives were also interned there. The work was endless and there was more information that we collected than we knew what to do with. I was one of several senior intelligence analysts on the task force. Succeeding and hungry for more, I volunteered for other assignments. I began to collect key information on HVD's and their relationship with their families and with other detainees. I was able to collect information on Saddam and others regarding their financing future terrorist attacks, hunger strikes, and even treason by US military officials holding key command positions. Still dealing with anxiety yet maintaining functionality due to the addiction of the job, I became increasingly paranoid. One commander was threatening to throw me off the base and out of Iraq because he stated I was improperly collecting and reporting information. He began a smear campaign and I could not understand why. Later I found out much of the information I collected on an assignment linked him and several of his staff, implicating them of aiding and abetting the enemy. He was later charged, tried, imprisoned, and stripped of his rank and retirement.

I was 10 months into this Iraqi gig when an assignment came that stretched me beyond my moral borders. I was asked to infiltrate a female naturalized American contractor from Iran. She was a translator who had been suspected of being an Iranian intelligence mole. My job was to befriend her and learn what I could by tracking her patterns of life and report on them to an Army contact assigned to CID. I began to ask her to join me and some of the other folks I work with to lunch. It became a common practice. She began to show up at unusual times at my workshop wanting to have dinner as well. Group sessions waned, and I found myself going to dinner alone with her. I was able to learn about where she came from, where her family was from in Iran, where her brother lived, and how she became a translator. Once a week, I would meet up with the CID agent and provide her with the collected information. Several weeks later, I found myself struggling with my moral behavior. I was married to a wonderful wife whose voice rang in my mind every day of how she said, "I will wait for you." I could not escape the love my wife had for me, yet I was feeling drawn to this girl I was collecting information from. I realized what was happening. This is what we call a "honeypot" in the intelligence community. I pulled myself together and took notes of everything that had been happening that year. It was like pages coming out of a Tom Clancy spy novel. In the intelligence community a "honeypot" is a girl setting up an intelligence operative to collect information from him, what he does, what he has reported on and his family and career, etc. They use their beauty and skills at all cost to collect what they can. This girl began to take a personal liking to me and I began to get uncomfortable. I saw that I was losing control of the assignment and of my feelings.

September of 2006 came, and I went to my boss. I told him that I needed to be reassigned for a change of scenery. I felt my family needed me closer to them and asked if he had anything state-side. I also went to my CID handler and told her she had to find someone else to report on this assignment as it was getting out of my control. I had never cheated on my wife and I was not going to start acting like some James Bond wannabe having spy girlfriends all over the world. At this point, I realized that I had lost all my spiritual bearings. I had no faith. I was running from one addiction to another, mostly success and money. I did not want to add women to it. That same month my boss found me an assignment in Tampa, Florida working for the Special Operations Command (SOCOM). I left just two weeks after my moral awakening. Upon my leaving, the person of interest I had been collecting on moved to some other guy. I ran into him a couple of years later and found out that he was another intelligence professional like myself and figured that she was his honey-pot without him ever knowing it.

Chapter 13

THE DARKER SIDE
("You Have To Come Home!")

"Good morning General Brown. My name is Will Cunningham and I am a senior intelligence analyst assigned to Trans-National Intelligence Team 1." "Good morning. Mr. Cunningham, what do we have going on today," Gen. Brown replied.

"Sir, our team has been tracking senior al-Qaeda operatives in the western Pakistan region known as the FATA (Federal Administer Tribal Area). Information from this area has been transmitted and collect from Tehran."

This was a normal morning for me, briefing General Brown or his second in command, General Scott, on foreign fighter movement across trans national boundaries and activity of key senior AQ operatives around the world. My new job at SOCOM was a senior intelligence analyst on Trans-National Intelligence Team 1. We were in charge of reporting on all pertinent collection of top tier senior al-Qaeda leaders. We had a list of about five leaders ranging from Usama bin Laden to a couple of his key operatives in Iran, Turkey and Europe. I was really at the peak of my career working here. I loved the job. I had access to the most highly classified platforms in the world. I had my hands on knowledge that no one in the world would ever know about with the exception of a handful of people. I was briefing high profile dignitaries and making a name for myself. Afghanistan and Iraq were behind me. I could visit with my family a couple of times a month and made a great friend in Tampa, Jeff Crouse. Life seemed to be normalizing for me. My little brother was kind enough to let me live with him for a short time until I was able to secure an apartment and eventually rent a house to move my family down to Tampa. That was the plan anyway.

I spent the later part of 2006 and the first part of 2007, working at SOCOM tracking senior AQ members all over the world. Jeff and I laughed about how we were saving the world. Jeff was a great guy. He was about five years older and a little wiser than I, as well as a war hero. He was a part of the Operation Nifty Package. Operation Nifty Package was a specialized team made up of Seals, Marines and Army Rangers that parachuted into Panama's main airport and captured the Panamanian dictator, Manuel Noriega, for war crimes and rigging the elections. Noriega placed himself in the country's highest seat through a military coup and stayed there for years, placing who he wanted in power.

Jeff took a team of military operators into Noriega's palace to find him. He was instead at church in the city. I remember one night hearing this story of how Jeff dropped into Panama. I was sitting at his dining room table and he pulled out two short glasses and mixed us a drink of whiskey and coke. As we were sipping on our drink he asked me if I knew what the monogram on the glasses meant. I said no. He then told me the story of how he pulled them from Noriega's home when they invaded Panama. Jeff and I would spend every Friday together having a couple of beers and eating at O'Brian's, a popular place for us intel guys to hang out.

As time went on, I felt the need to do more than I was doing. I felt that I needed a change of pace. Amy and the kids were not ready to move to Tampa, so I began to consider other opportunities. A former co-worker of mine asked me to check out a new contracting firm that was doing a great deal of dark operations, so I did. Before I knew it, I was packing up my desk and joining this other defense contracting firm. I didn't have to go far because it was also in Tampa, and I worked with the Special Operations Command on several initiatives.

Intelligence agencies only tell you what they want you to know. They only want to appease you enough with spy jargon so that you don't ask for more. The truth is there is always a darker side, a much darker side.

There is a section called Special Activities Division (SAD). Their jobs are primarily covert, hence the term "special activities." Just allow your mind to wander and you can probably guess that it is "anything can happen, if you find the money for it."

In the government world, funding is key. If an agency is awarded a million or billion dollars to fight the war on terror, then out of that seed is born a tree with many branches. Many businesses and contracting firms are also born from that seed. Some of these businesses are used as SAD elements to provide a service or operation. My new firm was tasked to learn new ways of man hunting. We were assigned a known AQ target list in a hostile failed state and began the search to find our targets.

I knew that this job was going to be different than any other job. In my interview I was told that I had to write a white paper on being placed in a hostile country and figure out how to get out without any money or resources. We had to do this with complete anonymity of who we were and what we were doing there. Since I knew a lot about the FATA and what goes on in that region, I used that location as my subject place in my white paper.

My job as a senior analyst was to plan, track, monitor and write about intelligence collection methods as related to man-hunting. The problem was that there was no experimenting. We had live subjects and targets and regional barriers we had to overcome. After working there for a week and getting my feet wet, I was assigned to close out an operation outlet in New York. While we were in the airport in DC I got a phone call from my wife. "William, you have to come home. One of our children has attempted suicide." My flesh went white. I sat down and ask what happened. She began to tell me that they found my son in a bathroom in another state. He had hung himself. He was working at one of our training facilities and was given alcohol by a worker. He was also given meth and who knows what else. He got caught and fired and when he left, he decided to take his life. An airport security guard went into the bathroom and found him hanging. They got him down and resuscitated him back to life just in the nick of time. I was told that my son came to fighting, saying, "Let me die." My wife then said that he had been taken to the hospital. I told her,

"Thank God," and immediately made arrangements to fly to the mid-west where my child was being treated.

Once I arrived in New Mexico I was met by a gentleman in his late 60's. He was a very kind, caring person and showed me great encouragement. He worked at the same facility as my son and had gotten to know him a little bit. When he heard what had happened and that my son was in the hospital he got into our company Cessna and flew to the hospital to be with him and eventually meet up with me.

I spent the next two weeks waiting for the physicians to release my child back into my care. We flew home to Asheville together where I began working from in order to spend some time with my family. As hard as it may have seemed, we as a family needed to move on, pressing forward to put things behind us. My child eventually recovered, and I went back down to Tampa to get re-engaged to work a new problem. The 10-hour drive down to Florida cornered my mind to recount all that was going on in my life and in my family's life. I realized that my family was missing an important piece of their life...ME! The problem was, I struggled with the fact that I was living two different lives.

On the one hand, I wanted so desperately to be home playing with my kids, loving on my wife and enjoying the Blue Ridge Mountains. It had been four years since I was home for any length of time. My family suffered greatly. I was a husband and a father missing in action. My wife and my kids needed me. On the other hand, I was living the life of "Will the Thrill" Cunningham. I have traveled to multiple countries, conducted hi-speed operations with elite special forces, collected some of the country's most sensitive secrets, and hunted down the world's most high valued targets. I truly struggled with the morality of it all. I rationalized it by saying what I do is and will change the world for the greater good. My family suffered, and yet I would move on to the next operation.

Over the next year and half, we conducted technical operations directly related to man hunting in East Africa. Our focus was on a small, growing al-Qaeda cell called "al-Shabab." They were virtually silent, but controlled much of the eastern African coast to include a heavy influence in pirating and even politics. Operationally we were given a green light to hunt and exploit key members of the cell. Neutralizing would be done through another agency. Much of the focus was the result of a war that had been going on in Mogadishu.

The current government was known as the Transitional Federal Government (TFG) and they were receiving heavy opposition from an aggressively violent group called the Islamic Courts Union (ICU). It was the ICU that welcomed splinter groups like al-Shabab. Another problem that complicated the matter was the TFG opposition also reported that TFG sympathized with Islamic extremists. Not only were there internal conflicts in the government, but additionally the US and UN concerns were escalating due to the myriad of Somali pirates working off the coast. Countless transport ships were being hi-jacked and held for millions in ransom which would end up funding al-Qaeda and other Islamic extremist activities.

Our team conducted numerous operations working with US Marshalls, Special Operations Command, other governmental agency personnel and allied counterparts. We were given a green light to do just about anything that we needed to do if there was funding available. However, the work began to take a toll on me. Not being with my family didn't help and always looking over my shoulder was a growing condition of paranoia. Although I felt like I was good at what I did, I was getting sick of doing it. At the end of 2008, I decided to find another opportunity. Our operations were becoming questionable and risky, and I began to have a moral conflict. I found another position working for another government organization in Northern Virginia. It sounded like a great gig. Three months on overseas in Afghanistan or Iraq and three months off back in the States where I could be with my family. I jumped at the opportunity and made my way out.

Chapter 14

F.O.C.

I was sitting before a retired Marine in a secure building outside the Naval Surface Warfare Center in Northern Virginia. My arms were riddled with taped cotton swabs and needle pricks from an afternoon of running from doctor's offices to get cleared to travel back overseas. My new boss, Rick, a retired Marine, was instructing me to drive up to DC and apply for an Afghan visa at their consulate office. "Will, I had you slated for Iraq, but we have a severe problem in Afghanistan. The lead operator in country has not successfully set up the JEFF operations in the three months that we've been there. We need you to get your gear together, get over there, tell him he is no longer needed and set up operations."

JEFF was a 75 million-dollar government program run by the Department of the Navy to place combat forensic labs in hostile zones to collect valued information resulting in actionable intelligence. It stood for Joint Expeditionary Forensic Facility. I was hired as an operations lead, which entailed me going over and setting up the mobile facility and house it with scientist to conduct biometric collection on the battle field. The collections efforts would then lead to intelligence which would lead to a kinetic or non-kinetic strike on a high valued target.

It was January 2009. One day before my youngest son's birthday. I had landed in Bagram Air Field and was greeted by the guy that I had to fire and send back to the US for re-assignment. After a couple of hours of getting settled in and being shown around, I mentioned to Peter (the guy I was relieving) that he had three days to show me everything that was going on in country and then he would need to pack up and head back to Dahlgren. I didn't make a big deal out of it but he did. He wanted to know why. All I could say was, "Peter, the government has spent hundreds of thousands of dollars in these three months and has not gotten anywhere. He tried to explain all the relationships he was building, but that still didn't answer the question why the mobile lab was not set up. I realized why he did not move forward with this project once I got to his office. He had set up an office with the very client we were to be supporting and he had gotten too comfortable.

The rest of the week, I got to know the military clients we were supporting as well as the crew that we hired who had been waiting around for work for the last three months. The night before Peter left, I decided to set a precedent. I was the Ops Lead in country for a multi-million-dollar contract. There was a war going on inside Afghanistan, Washington, and the minds of the American and Afghan people. When I placed Peter on the plane the next day, I turned to our lead scientist on ground and told him to get the crew together. I wanted to have a meeting with everyone. Six of us gathered together and I laid out a sharp plan to get operational. I told each person that I couldn't do this alone; I was going to need help. I asked them to follow the lead and watch things grow. Within three days we had the mobile boxes in place and began to set them up. The crew was great. For the first time in three months they began to see progress. I turned to my lead scientist again and said "Tim, tomorrow we are going to make business cards, go to every combat unit in Bagram, and let them know that we are open for business. We want them to know that we are here to help them with their mission of catching bad guys." That's what we did.

That night I made a call back to Dahlgren and reported that we are now "FOC" (Full Operating Capability). Two days later, we had an Army Captain bring in a bunch of items collected off an operation and we got to work. Forensics off that objective lead to identifying another person of interest which we reported. The program worked and within weeks we were flooded with more work than we knew what to do with. Even allied forces, such as the French, Canadians, and Dutch were using our services.

After several months of work, I received a call from the program manager back in the US. He had asked me to consider going north to a small region called Jalalabad. It was an Afghani territory that bordered Pakistan. This area was of special interest to the US government as it was the location of Torkham Gate. Torkham Gate was the modern day "Kyber Pass" connecting Pakistan and Afghanistan. More importantly, it also connected Afghanistan to the FATA, where much of the Taliban and al-Qaeda were hiding out. Multiple classified operations were conducted from the small FOB. I was asked to go and set up a presence with a contingent of 3rd Special Forces Group. I was to take two other individuals and become an embed providing training and combat forensics on the battlefield.

We made the trip, cultivated the relationships, began to train the operators on using forensics on the battlefield, and then we were asked to start training the Afghan National Police forces (ANP). This was a problem for me as corruption was rampant in Afghanistan, especially with the ANP. Nonetheless, we did it and were able to travel throughout the city incognito to train many of their Afghani detectives. Interestingly enough, we also began to get attacked more often as well. Our side of the base housed Special Forces on one side of the air strip and Other Government Agencies (OGA) on the other side. Most of the attacks were coming from the other side of our compound over the wall. We would get small arms fire and then mortar rounds would come in. One night we received 13 rounds in an hour. It was nerve racking. I pretty much said my last prayer as men on my compound were running about screaming, "Incoming! Take cover!" I put on my Kevlar helmet and vest, climbed under my bunk and put ear plugs in. If I was going to die, I didn't want to hear it. Round after round would come over our back wall and right into our compound. As I began to count them, I tried to figure out where they were landing by the sound of the blast and felt like they were closing in. In my mind it was a matter of moments before my life would end. I was simultaneously pondering what in the hell am I here for and asking God why I would die like this. I pulled out from underneath my bunk, grabbed pictures of my wife and kids, crawled back under my bunk, and cried as several more rounds came in. Within the next few moments, I heard screaming coming from the hallway and realized it was one of my team members. After pulling myself together I went to seek him out to see if he was safe or not. He was. He was just trying to get everyone out to a safer place.

The attack had stopped, and we would eventually try to bed down and get some sleep. At this point, I was living in constant anxiety. Week after week we would have smaller attacks. Even when I traveled to another location for assignment we would get attacked. It became more and more real to me when we lost three other contractors on separate occasions from mortar attacks coming across the FOB. Every day I woke up wondering if today was the day that I would die. I teased myself by saying, "I am just a dead man walking." I had no problem pushing the anxiety aside while performing operations throughout the day. It was more when I would try to go to sleep that I would experience a heightened sense of anxiety.

Our presence there made a difference for the operators that we serviced. We would end up working with and training three separate SF groups that came through. After about nine months of operations we were told to shut down due to a realignment of the mission in country. The guys on my team couldn't wait to get out of there. I ended up on the compound by myself for two or three weeks because the rest of my team requested to "get the heck out of Dodge." It took a lot of networking, convincing, borrowing, stealing and trading in favors to get help to ship out four million dollars' worth of equipment. But the job got done and in 2010 I headed back to the States.

The job was supposed to be three months on and three months off but it never turned out that way because we could not keep people long enough in a combat zone. So, I spent another year and half away from my family. When I got back to the States, I spent a couple of weeks home before I had to go back up to Virginia to work. I rented an apartment with three other guys and worked on a team for other JEFF programs. Within two months, I was asked to go to Iraq to a remote base to take over as ops lead.

Kalsu, Iraq is located in the dead center of Iraq and was riddled with mixed problems. This place was the original Babylon. It was the place where Alexander the Great died and now had both Shia and Sunnis fighting amongst themselves. When Hussein was in charge, it was believed he funneled nuclear weapons through the area. It is made up of slums now and had a heavy infiltration of al-Qaeda extremists. One month after arriving, we had a large suicide bomber penetrate the area in front of a police station that I was supposed to be visiting but had chosen not to go for another week. It killed 45 people. Kalsu was one of the loneliest places to work in. I was there for four months and was able to rotate out back to the US.

Chapter 15

THE ONLY THING YOU CAN DO TO HELP YOURSELF IS TO CHANGE YOUR LIFE

A couple of weeks after getting back to Dahlgren in August of 2010, I received a phone call from the intelligence oversight committee. They wanted to interview me for the work that I had done three years before. I was scheduled for an October interview. I spent the next few months going over in my head what was going on. I came to the realization that the government contracting firm that I was working for was conducting unfunded operations, which meant that they were conducting unsanctioned operations. What happened was our contract expired with the governmental agency we were supporting, and we were waiting for the next round of funding. Instead of waiting, we continued to do operations which red-flagged executive members in Congress. The real problem was not the funding; it was that we were providing actionable results and a couple of intelligence agencies were using our collections to conduct operations.

A couple of months after the interview, I received notification that my clearance would be suspended until the matter could be cleared up. I was grounded from traveling and was reassigned to a 21-million-dollar intelligence contract to recruit subject matter experts (SMEs), get them trained, and send them out to the field. This would last for another year as I waited for reinstatement.

During this period, I figured that I would focus on recruiting the best SMEs and ensure this program was a success. However, after a couple of months went by I started to wonder how long it would be before I got the green light to deploy again. I began to make calls and investigate my status. No one seemed to have an answer and I was redirected to a different office.

Another month went by and then another. My co-workers and supervisor were beginning to assume certain accusations about me that were not true. Friends seemed to distance themselves and others seemed to marginalize my capabilities. I grew more and more paranoid, imagining that I was going to have to sit in front of a Congressional hearing explaining why we continued operations when we were not authorized to do so. I began to lose sleep and entered a place of depression. I began to believe that I was being used as a scapegoat for some politician that authorized our operations.

Call after call was made and there was no movement on my reinstatement. What I could not understand was that I had been forth-right in all my conduct and had been very helpful during my inquiry. It's as if what I shared had vaporized. And maybe it had. Just maybe the work that myself and others performed were at some of the highest levels in our executive offices and now they needed to be filed away with lock and key. What bothered me more than anything was the fact that there was no explanation or status to my reinstatement. My entire career as an intelligence professional was being held up. I had held the highest clearance level the US government offered. I had spent years serving with and for Special Forces units around the world. I had helped locate and reported on some the world's most wanted terrorists. I briefed senior military officers, Generals and Admirals on intelligence movements and how they affected US interests. I had even provided intelligence statements to the POTUS daily executive summary. I had been doing intelligence work long enough to know how the systems worked and yet I was confused as to why things were held up for so long. After all, I wasn't a bad guy. I wasn't a criminal. I held the world's secrets in a vault in my mind. I was under such stress that I began to have severe physical problems. I couldn't sleep, and my sight began to blur in my left eye. I made an appointment with the doctor to get things checked out.

As I sat in the eye clinic in Fredericksburg, Virginia, Dr. Wang came in and said, "I have good news and I have bad news." I said, "Ok, just let me have it all." He then said, "The good news is, we know what's wrong with your eye and it is treatable. You have a condition called Central Serous Retinopathy (CSR); it is a condition caused by stress." I said, "Ok, so what's next?" Dr. Wang continued, "Here's the bad news. Your left eye releases a chemical to help balance stressful reactions and, unfortunately for you, it is too close to your retina. If I were to even attempt to operate, there would be a 90% chance that I could leave you blind, so there is nothing I can do." I asked Dr. Wang what could I do or was I going to have this issue for the rest of my life? Dr. Wang turned to me and made a very simple and yet the most profound statement that I could hear at that moment in time. "Mr. Cunningham, the only thing you can do to help yourself is to change your life and not be stressed about things. If you continue, you'll end up causing the same condition in your other eye." I said, "Wait a minute doc. You are telling me that I need to change my life. I am no different than the next guy or you for that fact. I pay bills, have kids, got a job, wife, and so on, and you are telling me to 'change my life!'" He said, "Yep! That's it. That's all that can be done for you. Change your life and the CSR will go away."

I had to call my friend Les to come and pick me up because I couldn't see due to the chemical they put in my eyes. I covered my eyes with sunglasses and Les helped me get into his truck. "Well, Will, what's going on?" I told him I was just falling apart. The Dr. told me that I have the condition called CSR and the only thing that could be done for me was to "change my life." Les started laughing at me and as he chuckled under his breath he said, "Will, I guess you need to figure out what that means." I said, "That's easier said than done, Les." He then said something to me that would begin to pop in me like popcorn on a kettle. He said, "Will, you just have to remember that God still loves you and has a plan for your life." Les would never know the impact of those words. I would even wonder why he would say such a thing, he was no saint. I knew he had great conviction and wanted to help me in my state of disgust. What Les didn't know is that exact quote was also said by my mother almost 30 years earlier as she and I stood over a ridge where I went over an embankment and almost lost my life. I was a little haunted by those words but was now seeking the comfort behind them.

One week later I had asked my wife to meet me in Greensboro at a hotel. It was halfway for both of us. It was August 2011 and it rained all the way down. She and I sat in the hotel restaurant and for the first time in years I began to tell her about my life - things she did not know I did as an intelligence professional. I uncovered for her the covered life I had been living for so long. I told her I was tired of running, tired of looking over my shoulders and I was tired of trying to reach for something more than what I needed. Amy looked at me intensely with her beautiful green eyes and said, "William, all I know to tell you is this, 'The Lord is my shepherd, I shall not want, He makes me lie down in green pastures.' William, the Lord is your Shepherd, you should not want. He has given you green pastures and all He wants of you is to walk in them." Amy went on to tell me how much she loved me and that she thought I was still worth waiting for. We finished off our dinner and went on up to the hotel room where I lay broken and in fetal position in tears from years of running. My wife lay next to me holding me until I fell asleep. The next morning, I got up and decided I would read some of the Psalms. Amy suggested that I read what another warrior wrote so she pulled out my Bible, which I had not read in years (I was amazed that she kindly thought to bring it to me). She reminded me that David was not only a warrior, but he was also on the run for many years and at times found himself in caves writing these beautiful prayers to God. That morning I began to refresh my heart, soul and spirit by asking God to speak to me through reading those Psalms.

For the first time in a long, long time, I felt a little hope. We finished up our time together and she prayed for me to have strength and wisdom. As I left the parking lot, it dawned on me that I had never considered what my wife had to go through every time we left each other. This had been her life for the last eight years with me leaving her to pick up the pieces and move on. Countless times I took advantage of our marriage and placed an expectation on her that should have never been there. I could not understand why she wanted to be married to me and why she loved me enough to work this out. She didn't sign up for this. All her life she wanted to be married and have kids and grow old together and I wasn't giving her that. I promised to, but I wasn't doing what I had promised. In my head, I kept thinking, "This is just life. It's just the way life is." Although I thought that, there was a part of me that didn't believe it. It almost became a household saying of mine. In other words, I began to adopt what I said and believe it.

Chapter 16

A PIVOTAL DAY

The fall leaves of orange, yellow, and red were covering the Northern Virginia road. I had just left the secured facility heading into town. I eased the throttle of my Yamaha FJR 1300 after shifting into fifth gear to a comfortable cruising speed of 60 mph. My beautiful day for a ride quickly turned into a nightmare. A couple of hundred yards ahead of me out of the tree line came up a helo and turned to the side where it's bay door was open. In the doorway was a sniper dressed in black. They commenced to lock onto me and released a shot. I heard it fly by my helmet. I switched down to fourth, throttled quickly, and turned on Colebrook Road heading west. The chopper redirected itself to follow me. This time it was to my left and behind as it came up above the tree line. Another shot was released. Again, a near hit, but a miss. I knew that I could not control the bike on these roads much past 85 mph. I also knew that if I could just get to Ferry Road I might have a chance to provide myself more cover with the taller trees and thicker foliage. I leaned into the curve, scraping my foot peg as I kept throttling, almost losing control of the bike. Another shot came from behind, missing me but flying through my windshield. As I approached Ferry Road, the chopper was rapidly picking up speed behind me. I ran through the light passing between cars, not even concerned with cross traffic. Cutting through the intersection I pressed on the brakes to jack-knife the bike to the right, allowing me to face left onto Ferry Road. I then switched down two gears to second while popping the clutch and throttling, causing the bike to tip on one wheel as I moved out of traffic, barreling down the road. The road soon began to fill up with trees to my left and right and I knew the helo was having trouble locking in through the tree line. I throttled more, reaching a speed of 115 and could barely hold on to the bars as the wind blew on me. I leaned down and barreled on as the orange, yellow, and red leaves rolled up while moving down the road. I was confused. What was happening? Why were these guys chasing me and trying to take me out? I could only come to one conclusion. I was trying to be eliminated because of the operations we performed, and who was giving the orders.

As I sped down Ferry Road, I not only got fearful, but I got more and more angry at why the guys I worked for would want to take me out. As I got angry, the throttle of the bike increased, and I immediately awoke in a panic.

It had been a dream. My pronounced fears of losing my credentials and reputation were causing me to be overcome with doubts and paranoia. My fears were coming out in several recurring dreams. It would take me hours to rid myself of the anxiety. My lack of knowing what to expect from my inquiry and status did not help matters at all, it only compounded what I was already dealing with. Again, I would just sigh and say, "That is just the way life is."

Several weeks later, Oct. 31, 2011 became a pivotal day for me. It was two weeks before my life would change forever. I left my office in Dahlgren and walked out to my bike. It was about 42 degrees. It was 4:30 pm, and I was struggling with my own emotions and disgust of my life. I hated being in the place I was. I tried talking to God but felt like he wasn't listening. I just couldn't stand the idea of hanging on to something that wasn't going to happen. I was tired of all the following up regarding my case and not getting answers. I was tired of trying to dismiss anything that others felt I had done and was tired of my boss pressing me about what I used to do and why I was suspended. The conditions of my previous work did not allow me to discuss the details. That was classified and was on a need to know basis. I was under oath to never discuss operational particulars. And I didn't. That said, I struggled greatly with feeling a huge void in my life. I hopped on my bike, buttoned my helmet strap, and walked my bike out of the parking stall. I gently pulled out of the lot and throttled down the road. The next thing I knew the bike had thrown me 25 feet to the right and the bike itself went to the left. We were both tumbling down the road together. I recall cartwheeling over and over and hearing the bike do the same as it crashed end to end on the pavement. As I laid there, face up, eyes shut, pain in my shoulder, chest and wrist, I remember feeling that my disgust had reached its apex. I saw a glimpse of my life pass before me and I prayed to God in that moment, "God, if this is the way life is, just take me now! Or else I will roll over and get up and move on!" My eyes still closed and struggling with some pain, a minute of eternity went by me and I heard God tell me, "This is not the way life is." I opened my eyes and slowly rolled over and got myself up. I looked down the road and there was not a car in sight. I looked down the other end of the road and there was not a car in sight. I pulled my cracked helmet off and looked at my bike all busted up. I was in such pain I could not lift the thing up. I stood there bewildered and amazed. This road is always busy, always. I looked down again at both ends of the road and nothing. Two men ran out from the building to help me pick the bike upright. We picked up scattered bike pieces from the road and one of the guys put them in his car. I looked over the FJR to assess the damage and felt it was probably ok to drive back to my apartment which was a mile or so away.

Once I got to my apartment I took my clothes off and took a shower to assess how banged up I really was. I knew I had some cracked ribs and a messed-up shoulder. My nerves were fried, and I was trying to determine if I needed to go to the hospital. I chose not to go and took some Motrin. I called my wife to let her know that I had an accident and wanted her to know what was happening. She balked back and said, "William, I don't have time for this right now. We are really busy! I've got to get back to work!" She got off the phone, and I sat there dumb-founded. She thought I was pulling her leg. She actually thought that I was telling her a story to just get a rise out of her. I couldn't believe it. My entire life seems to be crumbling down. I felt I was just about to lose my life and "she has to go!" What about me?! After feeling even more sorry for myself I thought I would call my oldest son. He was in the Army and would surely understand and listen to me. I called him and he answered as if in a hurry. I told him my story of the accident and he asked if I was alright. I told him I was, then he said, "Good dad. I am sorry, but I got to go pick up my daughter. Talk to you later."

175

So, I sat there. I felt like Harry Chapin was singing that song "The Cats in the Cradle" about me. Again, I was dumb-founded. I was in complete awe that I had no one to talk to at the moment. I had it all: money, a family, a great job, a nice Mercedes, a nice bike that I could get fixed. Yep, I had it all but really had nothing. I was empty. Very empty and I had no one to talk to. That night, I opened a bottle of wine and had a glass, then another and another until the bottle was empty. My roommates came home and we finished off another bottle while we had dinner. I somehow made it to my bedroom and passed out. I awoke the next morning with a terrible hangover. My entire body felt like it was caving in. It was the worst that I had felt for as long as I can remember. I struggled out of bed wondering if I should go to the doctor and get checked out. I managed to shower again and climbed back on my bike to go to work. I figured that I could have a buddy give me an idea of what I needed to do and where to go to get things fixed.

November 1ˢᵗ, a day after my accident, I felt it was a new month and I needed to do my best to move forward. Still struggling physically and emotionally, I wanted to be hopeful and optimistic. I was mostly stunned from the previous day's events. I recounted what had happened to try and understand what I did or didn't do to cause the accident. I didn't really understand anything about it because it happened so fast. I am a safe driver and don't like to take too many risks.

I tried to pour myself into my work and track what was happening with the hiring of the SMEs on the project. Right after lunch I received a phone call from the security office and was asked what time was I planning on leaving. I answered, "Around 4:30 or 5. Why?" The security officer told me they were going to have me leave by 2:30pm because my contract had been bought out by another firm and I was considered "non-essential personnel." I fumbled around with some words and said, "I'm sorry, what time do I have to leave?" She told me again around 2:30pm. "You will need to process out and depart the building." I asked her another question, "What does non-essential mean?" She stated that it is a person who is not critical to the mission of the contract. Since there is another firm that has purchased the contract, they are making changes immediately. They have already assigned your position to someone else.

176

Again, I was in disbelief of what was happening. Here it is a day after my accident, and I am now being laid off or dismissed because I was considered "non-essential." I walked out of my building with some pictures of my family and climbed back on my bike to go pack up my apartment. I called Amy and told her that I was coming home and would see her in the next day or so after I pack up and finish things here. I boxed my belongings in my apartment, mailed them off, called my landlord to settle what I owed, and on November 2nd of 2011, began my eight-hour trip home to Asheville, North Carolina. Back to a place I called home but never spent time there. In 2004, my wife and I sold our townhome in south Asheville to build on some land we were given from family. We built a lovely, modest three-bedroom home on three wooded acres on top of a mountain overlooking the Blue Ridge Mountains. We finished the house in April and two weeks later I was working for the Defense Intelligence Agency getting trained to go to Afghanistan. From that point on I had not been back home, except for short visits. Roughly eight years had passed before I could really call it home.

That was 2004, but now it is 2011. The ride home was long and uncomfortable and allowed me to do some deep thinking; some "soul-seeking" if you will. I had recalled the past few years and wondered if I had taken the right course to do what I did. After all, I felt I was made to be not only a man, but a man that would stand up for what was right. I wasn't terribly ignorant; I knew that evil existed and knew that I could assist the process of helping mankind combat terrorism in the world. I wanted my kids and wife to see that I was a man that was not just going to stand by and do nothing. I felt strongly that bad things would happen if I didn't make a stand. This ride home was shoring up the life I made as an intelligence professional, an operational practitioner, and a strategic programmer. I had hunted down Russian Bear bombers, Krivak cruisers, and stealthy Typhoon Nuclear subs in the '80's during the Cold War. I had pinpointed and identified hundreds of highly sensitive sites all over the world while also tracking weapons of mass destruction moving from Iraq to Syria in the early 90's. I ran, planned, and executed concepts of operations to fruition, allowing assaulters and operators to achieve their objectives. I had assisted and targeted high value persons of interest to succeed either capture or killing to make the world a safer place in the early 2000's. And in the last few years, I had traveled and trained elite forces and clandestine agents in the art of man-hunting on the battlefield. I was 46 years old, college educated, had credentials, experience, and wisdom, yet I felt and knew in my heart of hearts that this chapter in my life was over. This door was rapidly closing behind me and I wasn't the one closing it. As I rode home, hour after hour, highway after highway, I went through my life and kept asking God what was next. I didn't seem to have an answer, which was unusual, because I always seemed to have an answer. Rightfully so, I had not heard the voice of God in my life for a long time.

As I was riding my bike up the driveway, I began to realize that at the end of this journey that my life was going to have to begin to change. Everything was going to be different. As I pulled in the driveway, I saw in large chalk lettering on the payment, "Welcome Home Daddy!" I struggled to keep my emotions intact, but the reality was it was what I needed to see and feel. Years of my life had been carefully guarded to suppress feelings of love and acceptance to ensure that I would not get hurt. It became a mechanism to push everyone and everything out and stand alone to protect myself from ever being hurt or experience feelings of abandonment. My wife, daughter, and youngest son greeted me with hugs, welcoming me home. They helped me gather my gear off my bike and we made our way in the house.

The next morning, I recall making a cup of coffee while watching my wife and kids get ready for work and school. I realized that I had not experienced this routine activity for years. My daughter and son pushed out, and as I was giving my wife a kiss good bye, I told her, "For the first time in years I don't have a plan and don't know what to do next." She put her arms around me and held onto me and said, "Don't worry about it, you don't need to have a plan right now. You just need to know that God has one." She followed with a light kiss on my lips and before walking out the door, she suggested that I move things around in our oldest son's bedroom and make it into an office for myself. It will give me something to do. She then walked out and I was left to myself to process all that was happening in my life at that very moment.

I was out of my routine. Way out of my routine. I didn't have a go-bag packed, ready to go and hit the road for another assignment. I didn't have a place to go. Everyone else's life was on a normal schedule. Kids were off to school; the wife was heading to work. I was just the opposite. I was outside my comfort zone doing nothing. No place to be, no meeting to plan for, no flight to catch, no mission to gear up for, no one to report to, no report to write, no one to contact. I was completely outside of my element and it was terribly uncomfortable.

That day was spent clearing out my oldest son's room. I decided that I was going to paint it and move an office in, maybe a desk and couch with a coffee table. Maybe put a fish tank in and have a place I can call my own. Before heading out to the hardware store to get paint, I decided to go for a hike to collect my thoughts more about where I was in my life and what was happening. We lived on a mountain with very few neighbors. Up behind us, the mountain climbed to an apex overlooking the Cane Creek Valley. My thoughts were to take a short hike. It turned out to be over an hour to the top of the mountain. My eyes caught a glimpse of God's creation that I had not seen in a long time. I was able to take in something important, yet hard to explain, while releasing or clearing out my head a little. I hiked back down the mountain and headed out to the hardware store to get some paint.

The next day, I began to prep the room for painting. As I was taping off the walls, my wife came down before heading out to work and said, "I got something for you." She took an iPod she had uploaded worship music on and placed it in one of those iHome clock radios and said, "Here is something to listen to while you paint today." I remember trying to tell her that I didn't need her to try to save me and that I knew where God was if I needed him. She threw her arms around me and said, "I love you, William, I just want you to be ministered to in your Spirit." She kissed me and headed out to work. As I continued to work in the room preparing it to be my new office, I was listening to this worship music that I had not heard in years. These songs of praise and adoration and songs of thankfulness, were so different. It had been years that I had not paid attention to words of this type of music. Frankly, I had not really heard some of these artists sing before. I had gone back to listening to hard rock music to pass my time. It was great workout music. It was a complete contrast to listening to AC/DC sing "Highway to Hell," or "You Shook Me All Night Long." I was somewhat mesmerized by the lyrics of these worship songs. As I was listening, I was taking in the words and how they were digging deep into my being. Something was beginning to speak to me. Something was speaking life into the deadness I felt inside. I remember hearing Matthew West for the first time that day. He was singing this song that was really making me think. It was almost like he was singing a prayer to God, and I was listening in and agreeing with him. I could not ignore what was being sung. Here I was, trying to paint this room and move forward in my life and I was being pinned up against the wall replaying this song to capture the full meaning of the words, the thoughts, the purpose of why he was singing it. I replayed it several times to capture the meaning. The name of it was "The Motions." Something was speaking to me so deeply that I could not ignore its message. Matthew West begins to sing:

"This might hurt, it's not safe
But I know that I've gotta make a change
I don't care if I break
At least I'll be feeling something

'Cause just okay is not enough
Help me fight through the nothingness of life

I don't wanna go through the motions
I don't wanna go one more day
Without Your all-consuming passion inside of me

I don't wanna spend my whole life asking
What if I had given everything
Instead of going through the motions?..."

I was captivated by the words of this man's song because it was the very prayer that I had in my heart yet could not express. I felt myself tear up with emotion every time he sang, "I don't wanna spend my whole life asking, what if I had given everything, instead of going through the motions?" I did everything I could to fight through the probing that was going through my soul at that moment, trying to roll paint on the wall yet realizing that I was rolling in the same place for the entire song and not getting anywhere. I was stuck in thought, processing the impact of how I had been going through the motions in my life. Not regarding living out daily necessities, like work and family, but more so how I had been living out my life for the last 10 plus years going through the motions of living without God. As I struggled through the processes of my thought life at that moment, and trying to overcome it through staying busy, I was aware. I was truly aware that something was going on inside of me. Is this what my wife meant when she said, "… minister to your spirit?" Not even a couple of minutes had gone by before I was aware of the fact that I had a volcano heating up inside of me. The song had ended and this other guy comes on the iPod and begins to sing a song to God, "Awaken My Soul." I had never heard of this guy or his song either. At this point, a slow eruption was brewing up within me. I broke deep down in my being, slowly breaking outwardly. As brokenness brewed within me, a third song came on by another group I had not heard before named Jesus Culture, and this girl began to sing, "How He Loves Me." I could not contain myself any longer. By this time tears were just puddling up and rolling out of my eyes. I could not stand there rolling paint on the wall and not go anywhere with it. Something was taking hold of my life, my thoughts, and my being, and it could not be ignored. I fell to my knees and cried out, "God, what are you doing to me? It's not supposed to be like this." I continued to pour out a few more tears. I was not in control of what was happening to me, and I could not get a grip around my emotions. I slowly began to pull in my emotions and resumed my painting while listening to more worship songs. It was clear to me that something supernatural was taking place within me.

Either I would fight it and try to be tough and not be moved by it or I would just let it continue to soften me. The rest of that entire day was spent listening to those worship songs and many more while I struggled through an easy painting task. What was happening was something that needed to happen. God was trying to speak to me. I remember years earlier, a friend of mine, Danny Lehmann, who has written several books on evangelism, once told me that he came to begin to know God through a Led Zeppelin song, "Stairway to Heaven," while on acid. I wasn't on acid, wasn't drinking, was not even listening to Led Zeppelin. I even thought that maybe it's the paint fumes or the depression from a job loss. All I know is that something above me, beyond me, and out of me was impacting my life within me. That night while lying in bed with my wife, I began to tell her about my experience from the day - how I felt like God was speaking into my life through that music she had given me. This was actually strange to her and to me. I was not one to talk about things much, especially about how I felt. I could tell you what I know all day long, but to share my feelings and emotions was something out of the ordinary. After I shared with her, she encouraged me. "Maybe you should pick up your Bible tomorrow and see if He says anything else to you." The inside of me was saying, "Amy, back off, I got this!" The reality was I found direction in what she suggested. I needed the navigation in my life.

Chapter 17

JUST AS I AM

The next day, I was up and running, getting my paint supplies together and preparing to put on a second coat of paint in my soon-to-be office. As I was gearing up, I found myself plugging in the iPod that my wife brought down before and playing the worship music again. Amy had stepped in before heading out to work and said, "Thought you might want this." It was my Bible. She placed it on the desk and gave me a kiss, then pushed out to work. Here I was, alone again, spending time painting, listening to this worship music and finding myself being cultivated in my spirit somehow. After a couple of hours or so, I decided to pick up that Bible she brought down and flip through it. I noticed all the different notes that I had written in it from years before when I was pastoring, studying, and teaching, the years that I was walking with God. Here I was trying to figure out what was next in my life and wondering what I was going to get out of this day. I came across a verse that I had underlined in Ecclesiastes 3:14 and I began to well up in my heart. Beside the verse I had written next to it, "knees, summer of '92." Tears began to flood my eyes as I remembered the moment I read that verse when God revealed to me the magnitude of His sovereignty and divine providence in my life. It brought me to my knees then in 1992. I was either in the middle of Bible College or was finishing up my last few classes when I read it while doing devotions. I felt the power of God come over me and went to my knees in prayer and thankfulness in '92. I recounted the moment in my mind and wondered if I would ever be back to that place again. I reread the verse. *"I know that whatever God does, it shall be forever. Nothing can be added to it, and nothing taken from it. God does it, that men should fear before Him.*" (NKJV).

I continued to flip through, looking at other notes, wondering what I should read when suddenly something came over me. I remembered what Chuck Smith, the founder of the Calvary Chapels, used to tell us pastors. When you have lost your way, when your compass is pointing in every different direction except true North, then go back to the book of John. It will get you back on track. So, I thought, "Ok… what the heck. I didn't have anything to lose; the paint needed to dry anyway. I might as well relax a little and read with hopeful expectation that something was going to happen to me." I really wanted God to speak to me, like I felt He was the day before with the worship songs.

I turned the volume down on the iPod and began to read. As I read, the words were coming alive in a way that compelled me to continue to read on, not just a few verses or just the first chapter. That first chapter alone told me that Jesus was a light and came into this world to be a light. I knew that I was in a dark place in my life and that I needed some illumination of some kind. In my mind, I just needed direction on what to do next. I thought it was something to do with work, a new career, or something along those lines. I continued to read and came to Chapter 3 and could not get off the word "again." Jesus was telling Nicodemus that a person has to be born of the Spirit, not flesh and water. I knew this passage very well, yet it seemed to be more alive to me than ever before. I questioned why He said "again." I knew what He meant, but I just could not dismiss the word. I felt like I was being told that something had to happen "again" for me. I reasoned in my head that it was probably just poor theology and didn't need to be thinking that way. I continued to read on and came to Chapter 4. The entire story captivated me. Here Jesus was telling this woman all about her life. Jesus finally tells her that the well she has been drawing water from will always make her thirst but if she or anyone would drink of His well, they would never thirst again. Furthermore, if we take the water that Christ provides, it will be like a fountain spring to everlasting life. Oh, was I thirsty, and oh did I want something much more than what I was drinking from. I sat back and began to take it all in. I was drinking from so many other wells and was always thirsty. My life was empty, and I could not quench my thirst. I had money, some fame or popularity, had good looks, health and status. I had the American Dream - 3 kids, a hot looking wife, I had friends, education, a home in the mountains with views. I had a Mercedes and new SUV in the driveway and a great looking sport touring motorcycle. I wasn't without. I had things. But I did not have what this Jesus was talking about. I was thirsty. Really thirsty. My emotions began to well up inside of me. I continued to read on to Chapter 5.

The thirty-eight-year-old man was by the pool of Bethesda and Jesus came by to him. He came to him even in the midst of a multitude of others. I did not know whether he was the one in the worst condition, or not, but I did know that he was in such need. And Jesus said to him, "Do you want to be made well?" As soon as I read that question, I immediately busted out with tears. The volcano that had been brewing in me over the last few chapters began to erupt. I did not only feel, but knew, that His question to this lame man by the pool was to me personally. Some may argue that I may have been reading into the text, possibly over spiritualizing or caught up in the moment of depression or like I said earlier, sniffing too many paint fumes. The fact remains, something was taking control of my life. Something was ministering to me more than I could minister to myself. I was dehydrated of living water, void of the Spirit of God in my life, the very breath or air of God. The very reason to exist. I was thirsty, and I knew it. I read that text, *"...do you want to be made well?"* and it was like He was talking to me.

As the tears poured down my face, I remembered that word "well" in the Greek meant "whole" and this is where I heard Jesus asking me, "Do you want to be made whole?" I burst out and said, "YES! God, YES!" I got out of my chair and laid on the floor crying out to God in prayer, asking him to forgive me. I could not even sit where I was. I felt like it was just a holy moment. I saw my life, my very being, like a bottle thrown down and broken into a thousand pieces. Shattered. I knew I could not put myself back together again, but for that moment and time, I knew that Jesus wanted to piece me back together and could. I then remembered a moment when I was 6 years old, before going into the children's home. I remember sitting in front of the TV in Columbia, South Carolina watching the end of a Billy Graham crusade. I watched hundreds of people go forward, responding to a call to change their life. I remembered the song they were singing, "Just as I am," and that I wanted to jump through that TV and run up to the altar for myself. At that moment, I heard Him call me, "Come William, just as you are! For I will take you all broken and beat up, insecure, abandoned, miserable, lonely, desperate, hungry, thirsty, filled with sin, guilt and worthlessness." I saw in my mind that Jesus was pulling all those pieces of my broken life back together. I prayed to God and asked Him to forgive me for running away. I told Him that I wanted to have that relationship again with Him. I told Him that I really couldn't live this life any longer without His help, and that I needed His grace and His mercy. I lay on that floor, in tears of remorse for over 20 minutes. I was shaken up inside.

After a while of crying out to God for my life, I felt like I heard Him say, "Pick up your mat and walk." I got back up in my chair and re-read everything that He had said and done in Chapter 5. What was interesting was the fact that the lame man never gave Jesus a straight answer (a yes or no). The lame man just told Him why he could not get in the pool. Jesus never put him in the pool of healing either. He just told him to get up and walk. I felt it was like I needed the same message, that I needed to pick up right where I was and walk out my belief, walk out my faith.

As I continued to read on for several other chapters, the word of God came more alive to me than ever. It was as if my entire life finally had purpose again. That night, like the Samaritan woman, I sat with my wife and told her what had happened to me. As excited as I was to pour out my heart to her, she was steady and solid about what was happening in my life. It's as if she knew it would happen. She took a moment to say a beautiful prayer for me that I would continue to grow in wisdom and in His might.

The next morning, I got up early and made some coffee. My 17 year-old daughter got up, and I made her a cup as well. She sat on the couch facing me in my chair, and I began to tell her about what had been going on with me in the last couple of days. I told her that I dedicated my life back to Christ because I had been running for a long time. She sat there tearing up and began to tell me a deep dark secret that her mom and her were keeping from me. She stated that she had walked away from trusting God with her life a year before and tried to tell me all the things she had gotten caught up in. A life filled with questionable behavior and flat-out rebellion.

She then said, "Dad, there is more." We were both in tears at this point. She told me that a month earlier she had left a party that she went to one night and decided that her life wasn't worth it anymore. She was going to take her life by driving off a cliff off the Blue Ridge Parkway. As she was on her way there, she decided to call her mother one last time to tell her that she wasn't going to be home that night. When her mom, Amy, heard her voice and what she said, she didn't even ask what was going on. She just paused and said, "Elizabeth, I don't know what's going on with you, don't know where you are, or why you are not coming home, all I know to tell you is that you have Jesus." Those were the last words my daughter would hear as she drove up the parkway and could not get them out of her head. She showed back up at home an hour later in tears embracing her mother and talking to her for hours. She decided that very night with her mom to change her life and live it for Christ. She went on to tell me that there was more stuff that she was deeply ashamed of and wanted to tell me. As she began to tell me, I said, "Stop! I don't want to know you that way; I don't want to hear anymore. Elizabeth, God forgives you and that is good enough for me. I only want to know you in Christ, never in your sin. How about you and I commit the rest of our lives to follow hard after Him." I moved over to where she was sitting, and we just held onto each other and prayed out loud, thanking God for what He was showing us.

Less than two weeks passed when my daughter called me one day to ask my advice. She wanted to apply to Calvary Chapel Bible College, the same Bible College I went to. I was not only shocked, but also moved with such awe that she would desire to go there. I found it hard to believe that God wanted to work in that way. She asked me what to say in her application process, as she knew she was not the picture-perfect female student. She had a sordid past and had just worked through a major issue in her life. I ended up telling her to just be honest. "Tell your story," I told her, "let the chips fall where they may." If God truly wants you there, He will make a way." She did just that. She told the story of her imperfect life and that she was not the model Christian girl. Two days later, the Dean of Women called her and wanted to go over her application and ask a few questions about her testimony. Elizabeth told her the truth about her life, the good and the bad. The Dean of Women told her that she was the exact type of person they wanted at the school. Someone that was real and teachable. Three months later, Amy, our youngest son, and myself flew Elizabeth to California to get her set up in Bible College.

December 2ⁿᵈ 2011, my oldest son showed up unexpectedly from Ft. Bragg with his family at about 11pm at night. I asked what he was doing here, did he put in a request to come home, and how long did he have? He said, "No I didn't, and I may have to go right back if I am called, but I needed to come home and talk to you about something important." My wife looked at me and suggested we go downstairs and show him how I turned his room into my office so it would give us a moment to be alone and chat. As I was showing him what I had done to his room, I asked him what was up?

He said, "Dad, my unit has been called to go Afghanistan. I am a little concerned as our unit has a high mortality rate and I am worried about where we are going as there is much Taliban activity in the region." I wasn't catching what he was saying. I told him not to worry about it, I had plenty of friends still over there that I could hook him up with. He shouldn't worry. He said, "Dad, you don't understand; I am concerned where I am at in my life. I want to make sure I am right with God." I took a big gulp and thought for a brief second. I told him that his buddy Ryan from Hawaii was here to visit, and he just came out of Bible College in England and would be able to chat with him about it. My son then turned to me and said, "Dad, you don't understand. I want to talk to you about it." My entire heart dropped. I had just rededicated my life to Christ three weeks ago. As I took another brief moment to capture some thoughts of what to say, I told him we could do that. Let's chat more over the weekend about it. I suggested we spend a few moments together upstairs before it got too late. He went on up and I stood there in complete awe of the moment. I got on my knees and began to cry, thanking God for the incredible opportunity to share with my family members the story of how God can take a broken life and redeem it through the act of forgiveness, sparking a life of faith.

The next morning, we all got up and Amy made breakfast. I decided to have a Bible Study in the living room with everyone. I asked Ryan to play the guitar and lead us in some worship songs. I picked up my Bible and went to the book of John. I began to share what God showed me and gave my testimony of being lost and now being found. We looked at Chapter 9 of John and talked about the man that was blind but now could see. We had eight people in my living room. I prayed for my friends and family and asked God to bless each of them. My granddaughter (my son's daughter) was sitting on my lap the whole time, and I tried my best to record the scene in my mind. It was a special moment that I wanted to hold on to. I still pray that God would use the moment to speak to my kids the importance of being able to see God and not wander around blindly in a dark world all their life. That same night, my youngest son, who was twelve, came up to me after our Bible study with much conviction on his heart and said, "Dad, I want to give you a couple of my games." He had been playing an Xbox game that I was not happy about. It is interesting to me how the Word of God will cut through our emotions and desires and set us up to want to be right with Him. I will never forget how God was working in his heart in that moment.

As the weeks went by, my family and I became more engaged with living out a life that was less about ourselves and more about others. We would volunteer down at the local rescue mission serving a holiday meal or handing out coats and scarves at one of their coat drives. We were going to church and my wife had met and liked the youth pastor at that time. Ted had been ministering for over eleven years at the church and she had been going off and on for several months. She was so impressed with him because he took time to reach out to one of our kids and greet him and then her. That impressed her, as she is naturally a more reserved person. Here is a person with a busy schedule and people all around him, yet he observes a family trying to navigate their way in a new church and he reaches out to them to make them feel welcomed. She would later introduce me to Ted who then took the time to take me to lunch and hear my story.

I had spent much of the new year of 2012 looking for work and getting my life in order. One of the first people that I reached out to was Victor Marx. He was an old friend from Hawaii and now an author, filmmaker and popular speaker. I had not talked to Victor for over 12 years, but my wife had been following his Facebook page and told me that she felt like I needed to reach out to someone and talk about what I had been going through. I argued with Amy because I didn't feel like I needed to open up to anyone else. Besides, this guy is too busy with his own work and ministry. She didn't let me off the hook that easy. Amy knew something about me that only certain experienced people could identify with. And Victor Marx was one of them. Victor and I had very similar upbringings involving highly dysfunctional family situations. Both of us were abused on many levels and both of us faced living with death always lurking at our door. We were both traumatized in such a way that affected us mentally. Victor faced losing his life when he was a kid after being abused. A neighbor threw him into a walk-in freezer, leaving him for dead. Hours later, he was found by a family member and nurtured back to health. He suffered living with that trauma for half his life until his wife Eileen helped him through it by getting him some help as an adult. He ended up publishing his story in an autobiography titled "The Victor Marx Story." Later a movie was produced about his story under the same title. I, on the other hand, was abused and would suppress it until I was an adult and was triggered by several life-threatening events that brought me back to my childhood memories.

I wrote Victor and told him about my life and what had gone on as a kid, as an intelligence operator in Iraq and Afghanistan, and how I rededicated my life to Christ after running from God for years. I didn't think I would hear from Victor, but I did. Victor expressed in a letter he sent me that he could not believe we had gone through what we had. He suggested that the both of us get together some time over the next few months to help each other. He gave me the number of a person he wanted me to contact and chat with. It was really a lifesaving moment as I still struggled mentally over many things and it just helped to tell my story.

I also called on my best friend in California, Stan. Stan and I have known each other for more than 25 years. He is the one guy in the world that knows me better than I know myself. Stan has traveled his own road filled with rocks and dust and has come to beautiful pastures. After chatting with Stan on what I was going through and how I felt like God was changing my life, he heightened his voice and said, "It's about time Willy! I've been waiting for you to come to the end of yourself for 20 years. Gees man! Don't you feel better!"

I also reached out to several other friends that I had not talked to in years. Dean and I were in ministry together in Honolulu. I called him up one day to catch up and tell him my story. Dean wanted to fly me out to San Mateo where he was pastoring a church and have me get involved. He was always such a great encourager. Deano has a gift that is very rarely seen in people. He does not judge, but rather sees the potential of where a person should be and points them in the right direction.

Brad Lambert is a friend in Oceanside, CA. He and I were directors of the Calvary Chapel Bible College. He oversaw the main campus in the late '90s, and I directed a small satellite campus in Honolulu during the same years. Brad and I talked off and on for weeks. He would call on me to see how I was and pray with me. Brad was instrumental in helping me respond to the calling (or maybe I should say "re-calling") in my life to follow Christ.

Tim Newman another pastor friend of mine, who is the lead pastor at Calvary Chapel Windward in Hawaii was another factor in my restoration. When I called Tim, he allowed me to tell my story. After I finished he made one statement, "William, all I can say is, 'There go I, but for the Grace of God.'" He identified with my pain, my burden and my long struggle. Then he turned around and thanked me and told me that He would not be where he was today without my support years ago when running the Bible College campus in Honolulu. I didn't remember, but I helped get all his credits together and gave him teaching opportunities, which allowed him to get his master's degree.

Each one of these guys and more were very instrumental in restoring me. Victor helped me identify some of my issues and went out of his way to support me, even to the point of paying for me to see a family counselor of his. Stan would keep it light for me. In other words, remind me not to be too hard on myself. Deano and Tim made sure that this was not judgment for me, but rather grace. It was the grace of God that led me to repentance. Yet, the most important piece of this re-awakening came from Brad. He may or may not even know it, but he was the one person who helped me respond and move to the next step. It so happened that my family and I would be flying out to California to drop Elizabeth off to Bible

College in Murrieta and we would see each of them, except Brad. Brad and I would connect in another six months on another trip.

I remember on this first trip, while dropping Elizabeth off to school, how excited she was to be moving forward in her life. I was also excited for her. What she may have not known is that I was excited for me too. I was also moving forward. Each connection I made with old friends was like turning a page of my life. We stayed with Stan and his family, and spent time with other friends we knew in Hawaii who had moved to California. My good friend Dan who was probably the best and most truthful worship leader I ever knew caught up with us and after spending time reminiscing about previous years, prayed for us. I have always thought that God heard Dan's prayers more than others because he just had the most sincere heart of anyone that I knew. It was Dan that taught me years before how to play the guitar. More importantly, how the pathway of greatness in the kingdom of God is through humility. We also ran into my Bible College mentor, Tom Mauch. Tom was a famous tennis coach at the elite school, Punahou, in Honolulu, teaching the likes of President Barack Obama and Astronaut Charles Veach as well as a slew of famous educators and politicians that attended school there. Tom was very good friends with Chuck Smith and would often catch me up on the inside track of how Chuck was doing. Chuck was battling cancer, now in his eighties. Tom was Mr. Encourager himself. He and I chatted a bit about what had been going on in the Calvary Chapel movement. Tom was very special to me. In my early years, he would help build my library, buying me the best books to use for biblical studies. I recalled years before that he gave me one book that was very rare. It was his Grandfather's Bible that he used in Sunday school. When Tom gave it to me, he said, "I want you to have this, you've been like a son to me."

Before leaving California to head back east, the family and I decided to go over to the college campus for a goodbye coffee celebration with Elizabeth. I had texted Victor and told him that we were there and to stop by if he could. He did, and we had such a great time catching up. He would cut up with the kids and tell me how beautiful my wife was. Before having to bolt out the door and head to another engagement, he gave me a big bear hug and told me how much he loved me. As he was walking toward the door, he turned around and stopped in his tracks and said, "William, God is not done with you yet brother!" I can't tell you the size of the frog in my throat at that moment, but it was large. Of course, he said it in his Cajun accent, which made it all the more memorable. The lump in my throat was growing larger by the second as I was again recalling something my mom had said years before, when I was 17, after flipping my car down a mountain. She said, "Son, God has a plan for your life."

This trip to California was a monumental journey for all of us as a family. For starters, it had been a long time since we had done anything together, so it was a great time to catch up as a family. Secondly, this was a big move for Elizabeth and me. She was moving forward in her life and I was being re-created. (We were missing Christian, but he had Army responsibilities.)

Before flying out of California, Amy and I went for a walk in downtown Westminster. We had been staying at Stan's house as his guest and just wanted to take the time to collect our thoughts and reflect on the trip. As we were walking around the block, I began to tell Amy how much the trip meant to me, and how I felt things were changing so fast that our lives would never be the same. We turned the corner onto West Hazard Avenue and I began to tell Amy that I felt like I had been struggling with who I was for a long time and after losing the contract position, I struggled even more with confidence. I told her that I felt like people never got me, that they always misunderstood my personality and intentions of wanting to make the world a better place. She sensed my deep struggle at that moment and in a very direct and firm way, she grabbed my arm and stopped me, turned me toward her and said, "William, I know that people don't get you all the time. I know that you often go into things and people get moved out of their comfort zone because you want to make things better. I get it that you just want to make the world a better place, and I get it that you struggle with who you are and why God made you the way you are, but one thing I need you to get is that *I get you*! I've always gotten you, so when you think that you are all messed up inside and no one else understands, know this, *I get you!*"

As I stood there on West Hazard Avenue with cars speeding by and this woman holding me and looking up to me telling me that she gets

193

me, I welled up and began to cry. I threw my arms around her and just let it all go. I am sure it looked a little odd, two people on this busy thoroughfare hugging each other in the middle of an Orange Country street. It was a moment that I will never forget. I realized then that 28 years earlier when I tried to break off our relationship standing in her driveway, and she said she loved me and would wait for me, that she got me even then. I could not understand why I never saw this before. She had waited…and waited and waited for me to come around. This moment with her on the street in California sealed a great deal of security for me at a level that I did not expect. I was ashamed and relived at the same time. It was also at this very moment that I saw another glimpse of the love of God for me. My wife reflected such a deep devotion in her Christian faith that it began to transfer openly to me. I was both torn by it, because I knew I was not worthy of it, and was drawn to it, because it was the only thing that made sense to me. I needed what she was offering even though I wasn't worthy of it. It made sense because I could not argue with her love. I didn't deserve it, but I had to receive it because nothing else worked. She showed me what grace was in the walk around the block, Orange County traffic and all. She showed me that grace changes things.

Chapter 18

YOU ARE ADDICTED TO YOURSELF

Later that week after getting back home, I decided to attend a men's Bible study that I heard about. It was called B.O.B, which stood for Band of Brothers. This Bible study was held at a diner in the morning and usually formatted as a time of fellowship and then a person sharing a topical message or devotion. That morning I had the opportunity to meet many men in the community that were willing to meet up at 6:30am for some breakfast and encourage each other and learn something from God's Word. Mike Quest was the leader of the group. He moved from Texas after selling an automotive accessories business. I made an immediate connection with Mike as he was a down to earth type of guy, yet a go getter. Mike expressed a deep desire to see men raised up to not only be men, but be men of God. After a time of sharing and prayer, I asked Mike if I could get a few moments of his time and share my story with him. He was the first person in Asheville that I sat down with and shared my recent journey back to Christ with. Afterward, he prayed with me and invited me to another men's Bible study in the city held on Friday morning.

That Sunday at church, we ran into Ted again. I decided to invite him out for lunch and just thank him for extending a warm welcome to my wife and son. At lunch a few days later Ted heard my story and then invited me to a men's Bible study group on Friday morning. I decided to meet up with Ted and go to his group. Once there, I saw Mike. He gave me a big bear hug and told me he was glad I was there. That day we were going through 1 Corinthians 15 and I was struck by the immense power of God's word impacting my life. Robby was teaching. He was a local banker in the area. Robby was dressed in business attire and spoke with a clear, gentle and confident voice. There was no ego or arrogance. He was allowing the Word of God to speak for itself without his personality getting in the way. This impressed me, and it made the time listening all the more valuable. It was a style of teaching that I was used to when I sat under Bill Stonebraker years before. When we ended the chapter, it hit me that God was speaking to me in verse 58 of Chapter 15.

"... *be steadfast, immovable, always abounding in the work of the Lord, knowing that your labor is not in vain in the Lord.*"

This was my problem for years. I was not *steadfast*. I was not constant in my endeavors. I had a hard time finishing things. I would start really well but not be constant, because I would get beat up and then switch to something that I thought was better. Life is that way for a lot of people, if not most. This world does not have enough men who are constant in their belief.

Being *immovable* revealed to me that I spent my life on dirt and not on concrete, I was not *immovable*. I often had a hard time sticking to my guns. I was re-learning some valuable lessons on being a creation of God. Being a Christian man in an unchristian world was not for the faint-hearted. If I was going to realize that I am a created being by God, then I needed to depend on He who created me, God Himself. I had not been relying on something that is concrete in my life for some time. Almost 25 years before, I sensed God speaking into my soul and heart when I wanted to get married to Amy that the only way my marriage was going to work was for me to be like a house with a good foundation, the Son of God. Christ not only died for all my wrongs, but continues to show me how to live. I was reminded in this Bible study while Robby was teaching from this verse, that Jesus spoke about this very issue of being *immoveable* in Matthew 7:24-27. He tells the multitude of people that if we listen to what He says and do it, we are like a man who builds his house on a rock where wind and storms cannot tear us down. My life had been a storm from the moment I was born. I just didn't know what I was going to go through or why. The point was that storms will happen and if I didn't have a concrete, immovable base to stand on, then I was subject to being blown over.

Additionally, I had no bearing in my life of *abounding* because I was not continuing on with a productive and profitable life that would not only result in something great for myself, but also for others. A question that I struggled with was, "What good am I?" The answer was clear - not much good to anyone when I make it all about me. I had a chip on my shoulder and God had been dealing with me to come to terms with it. I was not "abounding" in the things that were important in life, I was abounding in the wrong thing. ME! I needed to be *abounding* in the work of Jesus Christ Himself. He told us in scripture to do two things: love God and love man. I wasn't doing very well at either one. I only abounded in things for me.

Finally, I lost confidence in knowing that doing good or doing godly was never a waste of time. I needed to be convinced again that being godly was a good thing to do. This very thing was happening as I sat through Robby's Bible study. I was being convinced again in my mind that the track and place I was in was okay. The recent events in my life were being pieced together. Here I sat in this Bible study where no one knew the wreckage of my life, and yet, it was beginning to form into something amazing. Just a few months before, I was going through a series of inquiries that could have altered the entire course of my life and my family's life. Then came the motorcycle accident, my identity in the job loss, my period of brokenness before God and re-dedicating my life to follow Christ, the time spent discussing the "Higher Life" with my oldest son and daughter which allowed me to ask for forgiveness, and then meeting up with or calling many pastoral friends who encouraged me along the way. Now, this very morning, God was up to something more through Robby's teaching. After the morning's Bible study, I approached Robby and asked if he had time to listen to my story. I felt it was important to share with him how instrumental his faithfulness and teaching were. I shared with him the boastful life that I lived and then the broken life I came to. I left very little out and then thanked him for allowing me to not only share but also come to the study. He stood there and looked into my eyes with tears in his and said, "Wow Will, God loves you and has such a plan for your life." He then prayed for me and I just wept, not from sadness, but from a place of being in awe. I felt I was again growing in faith. It was a sense of restoration that was taking place.

For weeks, I would continue to go to that study, participate, and be refreshed in my soul. Everything seemed to be viewed differently in my eyes. I seemed to be growing a pair of divine lenses where I saw God always at work. I had a sense of faith about life again. I physically felt my life was transforming before my eyes. As I made a commitment to continue to stay in God's Word and not only believe what I heard, but applying it in daily living, my life began to change. Was this what Paul meant when he stated in 2 Corinthians 5:17 that if *"anyone is in Christ, you are a new creation, old things have passed, behold all things are new?"*

Each week, I began to re-learn more and more. Old promises of God began to come to mind and I began to recall major sections of scripture that were dormant. I had decided in 1985 that I needed something higher than myself to govern my life. I found it in a relationship, a person, and I made a commitment to walk out what I believed. For years I struggled with the ability to be one hundred percent sold out. Now here I was being encouraged about where I was and what I was lacking. The fact that the guys in my group were just as willing to receive and grow as I was, impacted me tremendously. They all were going through their own journey. These were businessmen, successful in their fields. A couple of the guys were going through struggles in their life, job changes, divorce, a bad year for their career, and teenage kids who were experiencing drug and peer issues. Many of these men never knew it, but they all became a building block to re-engage my faith. It is hard to mention every last aspect of their contribution, but it is noteworthy to mention nonetheless. For this very reason, I think it is important to say: people change people. God is a person, and He changes people. This is the very reason why He sent His only Son to be a person to show and lead others to Himself.

After a few months of being plugged in with this group, one of the guys suggested we all somehow give back to our community. Andy retired early from the sale of a medical device business. He was in his late 40s and had done well and was able to make a profit from his endeavor. He was also a champion cyclist who raced with many well-known athletes, including Lance Armstrong. Andy was really ministered to by our weekly Bible study. He suggested that we take what we are learning and go minister down at the local rescue mission, Western Carolina Rescue Mission. So, we did.

Robby contacted the director, Micheal, and got his permission for our group to come down on a Thursday morning and begin to share with those in the mission's program.

The rescue mission was the city's largest homeless shelter for men, women and children. It served over 97,000 meals a year, provided over 11,000 beds per year, and hosted a one-year drug and alcohol recovery program for men. Each Thursday morning, we would go down and teach the men, and at times some women, what the Bible says about life. After several weeks, schedules didn't permit all the guys to come and eventually Robby and myself were the only two that were able to attend. I recall early one morning sitting in the back of the mission's chapel having a conversation with God about helping at the mission.

My family and I had volunteered a couple of times before, serving in their kitchen, but this time was different. I was there with all these guys in the recovery program, making myself available for prayer or to encourage them, and heard the Lord speak into my spirit. He said it was good for me to be here. I told him I was glad to be here and be available. He told me that I was there not for Him, but for me. I told him that I wasn't addicted to drugs or alcohol and that I pretty much had things in perspective now. "On the contrary," He said, "you are in need of recovery yourself. You are no different than these guys that are sitting in front of you, many who have been beaten up by poor life decisions and by years of addiction." I then told God that I didn't think that was the case. He said, "William, you are in recovery yourself, and you are addicted. Your drug is you!" I sat there in the back of that chapel while Robby was teaching out of the book of James and realized that God was right, and I was wrong. I was no different than these drug addicts in front of me. I had the worst addiction of all, me! I teared up and asked for forgiveness right there in the middle of that message, in the back of that chapel. I left differently than the way I came in. I was not only convicted but also revived. I knew that God had been working on me for a long time. If I was going to step out and get involved, I had to make sure that my heart was right. He was going to make sure of it, as He didn't want me to make the same mistakes that I made early on in my ministry years with Calvary Chapel.

Each week, Robby and I would go down and share on Thursday morning with the guys in the mission. One day, Robby asked me if I would be willing to step in and share for him, as he had to be out of town on business, so I agreed. We began going back and forth sharing, and I felt God's hand move in my own life as I continued to give back. One morning after finishing up, I was walking out to the parking lot and ran into Micheal, the director. He was stuck in his car with a major back spasm and could not get out and walk up to his office. I told him to throw his arm around me, and I was going help him get up the stairs and get him settled in. Once I got him up to his office, I told him that I would call back to check on him and see if he needed me to run any errands for him.

Now, I am not sure why I did all that, other than the fact that God was changing me to be a kinder, more helpful and caring person. Micheal was so taken back by that act of kindness, that he called me and asked me out for lunch one day to just thank me and get to know me. He allowed me to share my story with him about how I journeyed through life with some level of success, and yet I had gotten derailed along the way. Another couple of weeks went by, and he called me again. He shared his story of how he ended up in Asheville from East Tennessee just a couple of years before. He was a famous basketball player at Eastern Tennessee State University in the late 80's. After college, Mike went on to serve as a financial planner and own a small real estate investment firm. He also became a minister in his church. Mike volunteered to be the director of the Rescue Mission in 2008 because it was going through a leadership change and needed some help.

As we enjoyed a meal together, he asked if I would consider coming over to help him at the Rescue Mission. He wanted to add to his staff and thought I would enjoy taking a break from the defense-contracting world and devote myself back to ministry. I chuckled and told him no. It wasn't for me. After a couple of more lunches and some twisting of my arm, I told him that I would be willing to give him 15 hours a week to help him out. I didn't want to commit to full time as I was waiting for a couple of projects in the defense world to go hot, and then I would probably have to leave. So, we settled it and there I was, back in ministry. I sat and thought, "How did I get here?" Just a year before, I was in Iraq dodging mortar

200

rounds coming over the barricade. Now I am working part-time at a local rescue mission. Micheal saw something or felt something that I didn't. I think, in hindsight, he sensed the hand of God working in my life in a real and genuine way, and he saw I wasn't scared to live it out. After about a year, I began full time at the mission helping change our city's mind about the homeless situation. As I began to get involved in the rescue mission and its operations, I learned that it was much bigger than any one person or team of people could accomplish. I began to pray and reach out to those I knew that might want an opportunity to help. As mentioned, people change people, not a method, not a principle or philosophy, but a person. Many of the guys in my own Friday morning fellowship not only contributed to my faith, but were always willing to help others.

Chapter 19

T. R. U. S. T.
Amy's Perspective

I was anxious to read the story of my husband's life, so I could get to know better the man whom I had been married to for thirty years. I knew that there were pieces of him I would never have access to due to the nature of his career in intelligence, and I was willing to accept that. I knew some of his childhood experiences, but of course not all. And I did know of a few of the early Navy exploits. I was so amazed at the change in his life when he finally came home for the last time and stayed I wanted our children to know what an amazing man their father was and is. And even more, how amazing God is to take a life that seems so shattered and scattered and bring it all together and then begin the daily unfolding and revealing of someone completely new.

What I did not know is how to answer for the grace God gave me to wait. I suppose some things you just know, and I knew we were meant for each other. I would not he me without him.

One of my earliest memories is with my mother when I was just a little girl about three years old. We were flying above the clouds on our way from Wisconsin where I was born to our new home in North Carolina. I turned to Mom and said, "I don't see Jesus anywhere!" I don't remember ever at any time in my life not believing in Jesus. He has always been very real to me.

My childhood was pretty ordinary in that I grew up with both parents and two older brothers. We were active in church and there was no dysfunction or family drama that I was aware of. My best friend lived next door and we had many great adventures together. Fast forward a bit passed baby dolls and bicycles, I did have a rebellious streak in high school. I remember sitting on the porch swing with my dad after a tough time and crying. I didn't think I would ever find the right guy for me. I was just 16!

And then as if on cue, I walked in to work one day and met my new assistant manager. I remember everything about that moment like it was yesterday! From that time on, life was all about William. He made me a better person. Then life became anything but normal, at least as I had known it. But I would not change a thing.

Out of the thirty years we have been married, we have lived under the same roof for about half of that time. The first year he was on the aircraft carrier stationed in Japan. There were schools and moves. We were married three years before using many of our wedding gifts for the first time to actually set up a home. Hawaii was our home for almost twelve years. Our children were all born there, and life was pretty good. Actually, life was a dream compared to what was coming.

Just before we made the decision to leave Hawaii, I had two very memorable dreams. In the first, our family was driving along the coastline. William was driving too fast around a turn and our son in the back seat was thrown from the car and was falling over the cliff toward the ocean and rocks below. I tried desperately to reach him and seeing the panic in his eyes I woke up. This was one of those reoccurring dreams. Sometimes I would be in the middle of washing dishes and it would haunt me even when I was awake.

In the second dream, I was preparing a Bible study. I have never prepared or taught a study, but I was striving hard on this one in my dream. I had an acrostic for the word TRUST and my scripture was Psalm 91. (*He who dwells in the secret place of the Most High shall abide under the shadow of the Almighty. I will say of the Lord He is my refuge and my fortress; My God, in Him will I trust.*) I easily came up with To Rest Under (His) Shadow ... and was struggling for another T. Finally, I realized the perfect word: Today. I woke up satisfied.

Both dreams have come back to me many times.

I had also read in Oswald Chambers' My Utmost for His Highest how in the dark times, instead of running to friends or books to find out the reason for the darkness or how to get out of it, we should be still. It may be that the darkness is His shadow drawing us closer to Himself as a mother hen might cover her chicks with her wing and draw them in. What a beautiful image. And isn't that what I really want?

Looking back, it's pretty clear that while I had no idea what was ahead, God knew and was preparing me. He is so good that way.

It would be eleven years. Our children were growing, and William was missing it. I remember one time when he had decided to take a job in Iraq. I decided this time I would push back and tell him not to go. He had already made up his mind though, so I lost. I couldn't make him see that while we were so proud of all he was doing, we needed him.

The highlights of this time in our children's lives would include drugs, alcohol, pills, attempts of suicide, tragic loss of friends, teen pregnancy, and complete disbelief in God. This was my world while William was off being a hero and doing really amazing things for our country. How could I hold it against him?

God reminded me continually that I could TRUST Him. He also made it clear to me that even though I couldn't reach my children, when it seemed they were falling off a cliff, He could. He is faithful and is able. I didn't have to have the strength or wisdom or ability.

We both had our very different battlefronts, and neither could really relate to the other. Many times, when he was able to come home between jobs, we would fight before getting in the house, or within minutes of entering. His favorite thing to do was to grab the broom or wipe down the trashcan first thing. Who does this after just arriving home from a six to nine-month deployment? I didn't feel like I was good enough. I have since learned that it wasn't about me. He lived in a 7 x 10 room they called a hooch. There was such a sense of urgency and no room for anything out of place or people may die. He brought it home, and we didn't know it at the time.

When he finally moved home for the last time, I was nervous, to put it mildly. I had grown accustomed to doing everything my way. I really didn't want him coming home and being "large and in charge."

He came home broken. And I loved him.

The man that had visions of great things twelve years earlier was now back home. We had survived the near collapse of our family. He had physically survived life threatening hostile situations, but the effects still lingered in his mind. Now what?

Transformation.

My side of the story is quite simple. I met William at 16 and just knew we were made for each other. Only God could have put that deep enough in my heart to withstand dark, lonely, stormy times that lasted for so many years. I knew he was worth the wait. We have setbacks and disappointments, but it never entered my mind that we wouldn't come through. I have a simple faith in a great God.

It absolutely comes down to TRUST. There are so many things still beyond my control, but God has never failed me. He has re-made my husband, myself, our marriage and to some extent our family. We still wait. Only now, we wait together. What are we waiting for? We wait to see God's glory in our lives and in the lives of our children and grandchildren. At the publishing of this book, we have arrived at the beautiful empty nest stage. We have opportunities available that we would not have imagined in our younger days. We are incredibly blessed with beautiful and loving relationships with each of our grown children. They all have warrior hearts, which should be no surprise at all.

"But those who wait on the LORD shall renew their strength; they shall mount up with wings like eagles. They shall run and not be weary. They shall walk and not faint." Is. 40:31

Teach me Lord to wait.

Chapter 20

WHERE I BELONG
(Do You Want to Be Made Well? John 5)

Thirty-eight years of running can create a weight on a man's life. I had not known anything else but to run when things go bad, run when relationships went south and even when relationships went right. Regardless whether there was success or failure, I ran. On one hand, I did not want people to see my flaws and felt that I would be rejected again and on the other hand; I couldn't handle the success of things in my life, because I could not feel like I was worthy of it.

From the time I was 13 years old, coming out of the Carolina Children's Home and moving up to North Carolina, I was on the run. I truly did not see what real stability was. My mom and step dad were constantly moving. Over the next 5 years, we would move into 8 different houses between North Carolina towns: Asheville to Mars Hill to Marshall. I would move another 3 times before joining the Navy. The only stable factor about the Navy was movement. I either had assignments or port-calls in 8 countries. My life was anything but stationary. The norm for me was pick up and go. I had a real hard time adjusting to stability. In fact, looking back on those years I ran from the idea of stability.

The Book of John holds a chapter that has profoundly changed my life and views in many areas. I have mentioned it briefly in a previous chapter, yet I wanted to close this book out by sharing some deep truths that I have drawn from chapter 5, and how the message then speaks to me now. Although the biblical story seems to be more of an antithesis of my life, that is a man stationary for 38 years verses me on the move, so there is the parallel.

I want to ask us to read it together and glean from its teachings. I believe there is a message here for every one of us, especially me!

John 5 (NKJV)
A Man Healed at the Pool of Bethesda

1 After this there was a feast of the Jews, and Jesus went up to Jerusalem.

2 Now there is in Jerusalem by the Sheep Gate a pool, which is called in Hebrew, Bethesda, having five porches.

3 In these lay a great multitude of <u>sick</u> people, <u>blind</u>, <u>lame</u>, <u>paralyzed</u>, waiting for the moving of the water.

4 For an angel went down at a certain time into the pool and stirred up the water; then whoever stepped in first, after the stirring of the water, was made well of whatever disease he had.

5 Now a certain man was there who had an infirmity thirty-eight years.

6 When Jesus saw him lying there, and knew that he already had been in that condition a long time, He said to him, "Do you want to be made well?"

7 The sick man answered Him, "Sir, I have no man to put me into the pool when the water is stirred up; but while I am coming, another steps down before me."

8 Jesus said to him, "Rise, take up your bed and walk."

9 And immediately the man was made well, took up his bed, and walked. And that day was the Sabbath.

10 The Jews therefore said to him who was cured, "It is the Sabbath; it is not lawful for you to carry your bed."

11 He answered them, "He who made me well said to me, 'Take up your bed and walk.'"

12 Then they asked him, "Who is the Man who said to you, 'Take up your bed and walk'?"

13 But the one who was healed did not know who it was, for Jesus had withdrawn, a multitude being in that place.

14 Afterward Jesus found him in the temple, and said to him, "See, you have been made well. Sin no more, lest a worse thing come upon you."

15 The man departed and told the Jews that it was Jesus who had made him well.

Honor the Father and the Son

16 For this reason the Jews persecuted Jesus, and sought to kill Him, because He had done these things on the Sabbath.
17 But Jesus answered them, "My Father has been working until now, and I have been working."

This story is so important to me because it describes my life, and I would like to believe many other lives as well. Here in this text is the entire life of William Cunningham wrapped up in 17 verses.

The first observation for me is that I had been <u>sick</u> for 38 years in my own life. Ever since the day I left the children's home at age 13, I have been sick of my life, beginning with my past, my family situation, my personality, my present situation, my future. My entire life was wrapped up in my identity as a child coming from a dysfunctional home, abused, abandoned and rejected. My past drove my future. How I thought of my father and myself dictated my life. I was sick. I know that there are many others that feel the same way. Maybe your years of being sick don't coincide like mine did for 38 years, but maybe you have been sick for a long time and you are looking to be healed. Just like this man and just like me. I ran to anything and everything that I thought could heal me and there was nothing.

The second observation I learned in this event is that there was a multitude that were sick, which included being blind, lame and paralyzed. This again was something that I identified with. I saw myself in all three categories. I lost sight of who I was. I was <u>blind</u> to the fact that I was a created being and fashioned by the hands of God Himself. He knew my inward parts and my thoughts. I was also blind and could not see the truth that I was in sin, deep sin, running from God; abdicating my role as a man, as a father, as a husband and as a child of God. All I could do is exist, not live, but just exist to survive.

Not only was I blind, but I was also <u>lame</u>. To be lame means to be without foot or incapable to walk. I was so lame! I had no footing in my life. I had lost momentum to move forward. At best, all I could do is drag myself to join with others that are sick, others that are blind, lame and paralyzed. There is a great verse that states, "bad company corrupts good morals" or in some translations, "…bad company corrupts good character."

(1 Cor. 15:33). Who I hung out with, became my norm and held me back from a relationship with God that I needed to have. In my case, I was running around trying to be something I was not, a "secret agent man." All those that I hung out with were all just surviving, they were all around the same pool looking for some type of healing and only very few were finding it.

Then there are also those that are <u>paralyzed</u>. In this context it is those that have some of their limbs withered and non-functioning. Again, here is another category that I found myself in. There were parts of me that I know were paralyzed. Gifts that were of God, or talents that were no longer being used, mostly because of sick thinking. Probably just as important, what part of me was I no longer exercising or strengthening, causing it to atrophy. To say the least, I was blind, I was lame, I was paralyzed, and it was a sad state to be in. It was a place of misery.

The third observation I gleaned from is one of the most important of all. It states that Jesus saw the man lying there and knew that he had been in that condition a long time and He asked him if he wanted to be made well. This verse (6) is so important to me and I hope to others. It shows me a couple of facts. Jesus knows our condition. He knows our every thought, our blindness, our lameness, and our paralysis. He knows my sickness that I have brought on myself, often through sin and yet, he still comes to me. What a display of mercy, and a demonstration of utter grace. In mercy, he (the lame man) could have been left alone unattended, left in a frustrated state of judgment. So it is with me, I was not getting something I do deserve, that is, left in my condition to be in a constant state of unbelief. He could have left me in a state where the natural law of sickness would take its course and judge me to death. Instead as he came to the lame man and showed him mercy, and I see after reading this verse, that He came to me, revealing Himself getting ready to ask me if I wanted to be made well. The demonstration of grace here is getting something he doesn't deserve. Jesus could have gone to many other people there in that pool area, but he chose to go to this man. Possibly one who was in the worst condition? It seems, from the text that many others were jumping into the pool ahead of this lame man and enjoying the benefits of the pool, but he was in far worse condition. Yet Christ came to him and him alone. There were so many times that I felt I was too far gone to receive help. Just like in this man's life, Christ graced him with His presence and He graced me too. I was getting what I don't deserve, the presence and attention of the Lord.

The fourth observation, probably most important question for any of us, is the question Jesus asked this sick man. *"Do you want to be made well?"* You might wonder like I did, why would anyone asked a sick person, who'd been in that condition of sickness for 38 years - want to be made well? Was it a stupid question? We are told He (Jesus) knew the man was in that condition a long time. More than likely it was a rhetorical question. In other words, Jesus and the man knew what the answer was going to be. Jesus needed the man to hear the question to answer it. What is astounding to me is the man never answered yes or no, but rather blamed the surrounding condition. He pushed the blame on others and not himself. He stated that there was no one to put him in the pool, because as he gets ready, another jumps in ahead of him, leaving him unable to move into the pool of healing.

This portion of the text is such an important truth to me. All my life, I blamed my bad upbringing, my lack of a good father and struggling mother. I blamed my family situations for not being able to be healed. My constant feelings of abandonment, my missed promotion, my lack of education and my lack of being a good person were all blamed on others.

The real truth is, like this man, I really had no one to blame but myself. I was blaming everyone, but never looking to what I was called to do. I wanted to be made well and I was looking to others to do it for me and not Jesus. Maybe there is another way of teaching this text, but what I see here is a call to take Jesus at his word. "Do you want to be made well?" Are you willing to pick up that mat or bed you have gotten so comfortable with? As for me, was I willing to leave the condition of my past, my unhealthy thinking, my constant state of depression and pick up and move on? If Jesus decided to put him in the pool with the intent of ushering hope to this lame man, the man would probably never have been moved in his faith any more than what was in his own heart. Many believed that angels came to visit the pool to stir its waters and heal those who went into the pool after it's stirring. The problem of this is that would take away from who Jesus was going to become to this man. He would become the healer for this man, nothing more, based on the reading of the text. Jesus wanted to become this man's savior. Whenever we have a divine intervention, whenever there is an event that is seemingly above our natural circumstances, then we must recognize that it is from God. It is heaven appointed and anointed to do something that is beyond our own capabilities. In these moments, God is asking or wanting us to do one thing, follow Him or better said, just obey. For this man, he was found sometime later in the temple worshiping God. This healing was meant for this man to be reconciled to God. He now worships Him in a way he had not done for 38 years. This leads me to another observation and the close of my story.

In the fifth observation I want to make, I felt it important to note what Jesus said and what the man did. Jesus told the man to arise, take up the bed he was lying on and walk. (V. 8-9). Jesus commanded of him something that the man could freely use, his will. Now we know that it was Jesus that healed the man, but what I find interesting here is that so often in my own life I have not acted with confidence to take up my bed and walk, whether it be in my personal life or my public life. Again, I had relied on the growth of others to carry me and never trusted my relationship with God enough to act in my own will to glorify Him. This has been such a tragedy in my past. I have had the very presence of God over my life and yet have ignored it by not relying on Him, but rather, relying on man or myself. This could never be truer than understanding who Jesus is and what He has done in my life, specifically in the area of forgiveness. Most of us understand that in forgiveness we can be free from guilt. This is what Jesus does. He takes the guilt away. I know that I have struggled with that divine principle most of my life, because although I knew that Jesus came and paid the price for my sins, clearing me of a guilty conscience, I would at times still be held back from being healed because I couldn't forgive myself. Here is really where the rubber meets the road. We learn in another book of the Bible that Jesus taught His disciples to pray and that when they pray, put the emphasis on forgiving others before you understand forgiveness for yourself (Matt. 6:9-13).

I essentially had to come to terms of forgiving others before grasping His forgiveness for me. I had to forgive my Dad and Mom for not ushering in a better world for us kids. If I could not do so, then I would be bound by my bitterness. It is much clearer to me now than ever before as I walk with Christ daily. I have learned this simple truth: we were all born into this fallen world of sin and we all will make fallen decisions; therefore, we really have one option, which is to understand that we need to learn forgiveness and love each other in spite of our fallen state. This is not an easy task. I am not saying we excuse away poor behavior that is correctable. I am not saying that we just throw peace and love slogans all over the place and walk about like hippies and be cool with everything. I am saying that we just need to understand that we have all fallen, and have come short of God's expectations and that it just might be the very tool of forgiveness wrought by love that brings relationships along the path a little closer to where God intends us to be.

It is an act of the will, and that is my point. This man willed to be made well. In 2 Corinthians 8:12, we learn a very simple truth about giving, yet the same principle applies here. Paul writes, "For if there is first a willing mind, *it is* accepted according to what one has, *and* not according to what he does not have." Again, this may relate to giving out of what we have and not out of what we do not have. The underlying principle is found in the act of the will. This man was willing to be made well. God does not expect me to do something that is not within me. He will do that which I cannot do. So, this question now haunts me from my past to my present. It haunts me in a good way. In any situation, am I willing to be made well and if so, am I willing to do whatever it takes for it? Am I willing to rise and move away from something that I have been comfortable with for so long and willing to walk in a different direction? This could relate to the bitterness of being brought up in a broken environment. It could be a sin we have been holding on to, a lack of forgiveness as mentioned earlier or even a path of success. It could be bad, unhealthy thinking that we have become comfortable with. Are you willing to be made well and willing to arise out of that which has been holding you back?

The final observation I would like to make is the result of where this lame man ended up. Specifically, the temple or more specifically, worshiping God. This is "where he belonged." (v.14). What I love about this event is that this is where this man ended up, right after this life-changing experience, a place of worship. Let me be real clear here, it is not the building, not even the church or room that you have to go to. It is the place of worship. It is where we all belong. It is the place where we find ourselves in the presence of God. This is the place where He wants us, with Him. In Psalm 91:1 it tells us: "He who dwells in the secret place of the Most High, shall abide in the shadow of the Almight." It is the greatest place to be, for anywhere else and anyone else will utterly and eventually fail us.

I have spent my entire life, as you have read it here running from place to place, relationship to relationship. I have gone from one painful moment to another. I have hidden behind doors as a child in fear of others and hidden under beds in fear of death. I have sought great things, like significance and recognition and yet at times I have also been comfortable lying in my bed of defeat and failure. The realization that I have come to is that being where God is, a place of constant worship, whatever and where ever that place is, is "Where I Belong."

I have been back home since late 2011. I have begun a new life after years of abuse, neglect, running from God and running from relationships. In these years that I have been back with my wife and kids in our mountain home in North Carolina, I have learned more about myself than ever before.

There is a great verse in 2 Samuel chapter 14, verse 14 that has captured my understanding of the heart of God. It is about King David who is stuck between a rock and a hard place with making a decision to bring Absalom, his son back to the kingdom. David has made one bad decision after another and now finds himself in utter despair.

It states: *"For we will surely die and become like water spilled on the ground, which cannot be gathered up again. Yet God does not take away a life; but He devises means, so that His banished ones are not expelled from Him."*

The woman of Tekoa provided this statement to David when he needed to hear it most. She revealed the truth about God's character that should never be forgotten. That truth is that God cares and still has a plan for your life.

My life was not reduced to water spilled on the ground; God has a plan when I am willing. How do I know this verse is true for me? I found myself working in a rescue mission, helping homeless people, feeding them and sheltering them. I found myself teaching and mentoring 3 times a week to men and women going through recovery who were caught up in drug and alcohol and other addictive behaviors. I have renewed my marriage when it was so close to failure. I have, and continue to cultivate a relationship with my kids again and have zeal to coach and love them through life. I have more friends then I know what to do with and can call on them any time, any day for anything. I have achieved personal goals as I earned my Masters and other certifications. I have been involved with great ministries to include wonderful area churches. My wife and I have found our hearts in Lebanon to reach out and support some 2 million Syrian and Iraqi refuges with transformational relief through the organization Heart for Lebanon. I have found myself working alongside other counselors to help counsel on a weekly basis countless broken marriages and lost individuals, and others that are sick, blind, lame and paralyzed.

Most importantly, as of October of 2018, my life and this verse out of 2 Samual 14:14 collided in a radical way that catapulted my faith in a way that I never thought it could. It had to do with my real dad that I had not seen or heard from in years. What I thought was a done deal, that is, the forgiveness of family hurts and moving on, was only in part. I still had the occasional haunting of rejection that slipped in from time to time. That abandonment feeling that would disrupt me for a few days, cause me to be cynical with others and dismantle well established securities in my marriage haunted me. In early September, I decided to check in to see if my dad had passed away and began to look into the obituary of the state paper where I thought he lived. I found him in a public record and he was still alive. All of the sudden I was overwhelmed with feelings that I knew I had sorted out, yet was blind-sided. Was this spiritual warfare at it's best? Was I in denial about forgiveness with my dad? Was it lack of sleep and grieving and guilt I felt because my wife and I were fighting? It all came to an empass. It was my wife that suggested that it might just be God refining us. Calling us to be holy not just live the average Christian life. God's holiness was haunting me, truly haunting me. Again, here is where the rubber met the road. She came to me a few days later at breakfast one morning and said, "You need to go see your dad and thank him for bringing you in this world and tell him how God has used every circumstance in your life to bring you to a place to have helped so many people." What she said shattered every piece of religion within me. What she was suggesting is that I go and tell the man that in spite of all that he has done, that he is still worth it all to God and to me, because God chose him to bring me into this world.

I was flooded with emotion and began to inwardly crumble in my chair. I got up and began to walk away in utter crushing but my legs were giving out. My wife ran to me to hold me up where I began to let it all go. I cried and cried, because what she suggested was the holiness that was haunting me. She was asking me to do something that was probably the most Christ-like act I have ever done. She was asking me to give up all my rights and privileges so that my dad can experience the same redemption that I have. She was asking me to demonstrate my love to him, in spite of what he had done.

Two weeks later, Amy and I prayed and decided to jump in the car and drive the couple hours to his house. Unsure if there was anyone there, with no number to call, and only the address we pulled off of public records, we knocked on the door. A kind lady answered the door and I asked if he lived there. She said yes. I told her who I was and she smiled really big and said, "Come in, I've been praying that one of you kids would come for a visit." My dad sat on a couch, yielding all of 81 years of age, on an oxygen tank and suffering from a rare lung disorder that is progressively getting worse. I began to tell him how I had him on my mind and then shared my heart with him, letting him know that I wanted to thank him for bringing me into this world and I shared how important it was for him to know that his contribution to my life has made a huge impact in the world we live in. I also shared with him how I surrendered my life to Christ in 1985 and wrote him a letter, forgiving him. He then told me things that changed my entire view of him. He told me that he had written me back and the letter was returned to him but he didn't know where else to send it. He also told me that he had tried to visit me several times when I had moved back to the states and was asked not to come around by my other siblings and relatives. I had mentioned something to my wife a few days before, this late October day, which came back to my memory. I stated to her in a moment of emotion that my dad never had a chance to make things right because of his own dysfunctional upbringing. Not only did he not have a chance to make things right due to a broken life, he also had the difficulty of navigating through other's hurt and hatred, mainly his kids and my mother's second husband. Again, redemption was not given a chance. Yet, here is how I feel that very verse in 2 Samuel 14:14 played out in my life. My dad was not and is not completely expelled from the fellowhip of God. Whether or not other family members chose to consider him an outcast, God made a way so that this man does not pass from this life without an opportunity to be forgiven, loved and assured of redemption. "God does not take away a life, but devises a means...."

... He devises a means... It may be that the very means that He devises is us. You see, the woman of Tekoa was a key to David's misery. She was the means by which God would use to minister to David's heart, to get him to see God and His character. And so it is for us. We might be the very means by which God wants to use to reveal his character. For my dad, I might just be a part of the means that God wants to use to have him see the character of God and even more, to see the love of God. The Gospel is more than just words to share, it is a life to be lived out in front of others to be a witness, a key that unlocks doors. All those years I spent running around doing those cool things for God and country, I did because others would not or could not. Whether it was dangling from helicopters taking pictures of Russian ships, or being pulled from one boat to another by replenishment cables or traveling all over Afghanistan and Iraq performing secret missions, I did it, because others were not willing to do it or could not do it. I did it because I felt I was the key to helping something bigger take place. I did not ask for these things, but they were the opportunities that lay before me and I needed to seize them to make a difference. Each time I did, I went in, all in, whether I was going to succeed or fail. The point is, you just might be the key to unlock someone's life. You might be or could be the very means to carry God's love to a broken family member, a spouse, a sibling, a friend, an estranged parent.

I could never have known my life would turn out like this. I didn't plan it this way, which is probably a good thing. Based on my early story,

I was not heading in the right direction. I was a runner. Running from the love of God and running from giving the love of God. Until one day His love broke through and captivated my life. So, I now find myself at much more peace with who I am. Learning to love God and love others, because He loves me and loves others. I am at peace where I am living. I enjoy how I am making a difference. And most importantely, like the lame man who was on that mat looking for a someone to put him in the pool and later found himself in the temple worshiping a God who truly had his life marked out for a reason, I too find my life marked out and find myself now worshiping God. I find myself exactly "Where I Belong."

BIO

A US Navy veteran serving honorably in multiple conflicts & wars since 1985 with additional time spent in Afghanistan and Iraq as a military liaison to Special Forces units. William is a graduate of Montreat College with a Masters in the school's executive MBA program.

After serving several years overseas in multiple countries in the late 80's to early 90's as a Naval intelligence professional, William accepted a ministry position as an assisting pastor of the largest church within his denomination in Hawaii. He learned quickly that the greatest asset to any leader is his assistant. He directed and navigated the ministry's radio syndication in 5 markets to 215 markets nationally in a two-year period. He additionally directed an affiliated Bible College as a teaching director. From 2000 to 2004 William operationally managed two separate businesses suffering from near failure to a steady profit growth by implementing achievable milestones, a follow-up system and great customer relationships. A call from the Defense Intelligence Agency in 2004 redirected William to serve as an intelligence asset to Special Forces units in Afghanistan and Iraq. Over the next several years, he would lead several operational components in multiple hostile locations, ensuring both kinetic and non-combative missions were achieved. In 2011, William assisted in restructuring a 21-million-dollar intelligence contract to be successfully bought out, allowing him to pursue other interest and spend much needed time with family. In 2012 he focused his interests on creating a better environment by volunteering and then serving as Chief Operating Officer and Major Gift Officer of the largest homeless shelter in Western North Carolina where he spent much of his time teaching and coaching life-changing principles with those going through recovery. William's motto is, "*Let's get caught doing good together.*" He has assisted the Director and Board members of the Western Carolina Rescue Mission in downtown Asheville with the management of approximately 2.5 million in contributions and hard assets. He currently serves as the Advancement

Manager with the Heart for Lebanon Foundation, a faith-based NGO serving displaced Syrian families living in Lebanon farmlands as refugees.

William is married to Amy, and they have three children. Christian who has two children, Hayden and Hunter. Elizabeth who is married to Kevin with a son, Knox. Blake graduated with honors in military training and is in the U.S. Marine Corp stationed in California.

William believes in lifelong learning. Aside from his MBA from Montreat College, he also is a 1992 graduate of Calvary Chapel Bible College School of Ministry (SOM) followed by a pastoral commissioning. In 2010 he received a Master certification in Applied Project Management through Villanova University. In 2014 he completed his requirements as a certified Temperament Counselor through Sarasota Academy of Christian Counseling; and is a professional clinical member of the National Christian Counseling Association.

William now has a Christian Counseling Practice in the Mountains of North Carolina where he teaches his clients to give their life away and leads a Bible Study in a local businessman's warehouse. To know more go to www.ashevillechristiancounseling.com.

He has been featured as a guest in the Victor Marx film, Triggered, where he along with special operators and a Medal of Honor recipient discuss their plight dealing with PTSD. To learn more go to: http://triggeredthemovie.com/

He also serves with the Heart for Lebanon Organization, a global faith-based humanitarian organization, where he donates portions from this book to help. Go to www.heartforlebanon.org to learn more.

William's passion is to see people freed from the very things that hold them in bondage and often invites them to travel with him to Lebanon to work alongside the people assisting the 1.7 million Syrian refugees in the country's farmlands.

References

i Keith Green:
http://www.lastdaysministries.org/Groups/1000086197/Last_Days_Ministr
ies/Articles/By_Keith_Green/Whats_Wrong_With/Whats_Wrong_With.as
px

ii Ronald Reagan Library:
http://www.reagan.utexas.edu/archives/speeches/1987/061287d.htm

iii Fury to Freedom 1985:
http://www.imdb.com/title/tt0205958/

iv Bucket:
http://www.army.mil/article/1662/sf-soldier-gets-silver-star-for-heroism-
in-afghanistan/

CPSIA information can be obtained
at www.ICGtesting.com
Printed in the USA
FSHW020128070819
60753FS